PHILIPPIANS

PHILIPPIANS

AARON ERHARDT

ERHARDT PUBLICATIONS

LOUISVILLE, KENTUCKY
2011

DEDICATION

To Seth Isaac Erhardt.
My prayer is that you grow up to be a faithful servant
of the Lord Jesus Christ, and that you never
waver in your service to Him.
May you be blessed in body, mind, and soul.

OUTLINE

CHAPTER ONE

CHAPTER TWO

CHAPTER THREE

CHAPTER FOUR

INTRODUCTION

P hilippians is often called "Paul's Love Letter" because of its many warm words of affection. One cannot help but sense the deep love that existed between the apostle and some of his dearest converts. Paul said, "I hold you in my heart" (1:7), "I yearn for you all with the affection of Christ Jesus" (1:8), and referred to them as "my brothers, whom I love and long for, my joy and crown...my beloved" (4:1).

> This is an epistle of the heart, a true love-letter, full of friendship, gratitude and confidence; it makes those intimate revelations of the soul's history and emotions which the deepest sympathy and mutual affection alone are wont to elicit. (1)

Philippians is also called "The Letter of Joy" since the words "joy" and "rejoice" are frequently used in the letter (1:4, 18, 25; 2:2, 17, 18, 28, 29; 3:1; 4:1, 4, 10). When one considers the fact that Paul was in chains, uncertain of his future, knew that some preachers were trying to harm him, and feeling the infirmities of old age (Philemon 9), it is truly remarkable that he could speak of such joy. The same is true from the Philippian perspective. They were poor, persecuted, threatened by false teachers, troubled by squabbling sisters, and sorrowed by Paul's situation, yet were told to rejoice. That is because the joy of a Christian is not dependent upon circumstances but exists in spite of them.

WRITER

The letter to the Philippians was written by Paul the apostle during his first Roman imprisonment. He identified himself as the writer in 1:1 and gave a brief autobiography in 3:5-6. Furthermore, many of the post-apostolic writers identified Paul as the writer, including Polycarp, Irenaeus, Ignatius, Clement of Alexandria, Tertullian, etc.

Although Timothy is mentioned in 1:1, we should not view him as an equal co-writer. The consistent use of "I" rather than "we" and the reference to Timothy in the third person (2:19) support this view. Paul often included the names of certain companions who were present with him at the time of the writing and known by the recipients.

Timothy may have served as Paul's secretary, that is, the one who transcribed the apostle's dictation (see Romans 16:22). In such cases, Paul would sign the letter near the end for authenticity (1 Corinthians 16:21; Colossians 4:18; 2 Thessalonians 3:17). Some, however, believe that Epaphroditus wrote the letter for Paul since some Greek manuscripts have subscriptions with his name.

Paul earnestly desired to preach the gospel in Rome (Romans 1:15). That desire was fulfilled in a most unconventional manner—the preacher went there as a prisoner! However, this letter made it clear that God was at work all along.

Ruins of ancient Philippi.

Ruins of ancient Philippi.

Amphitheatre in Philippi.

DATE & PLACE

The letter to the Philippians was written near the end of Paul's first Roman imprisonment around A.D. 62. It was probably the latest of the four so-called prison letters. Paul's references to the imperial guard (1:13) and to Caesar's household (4:22), along with the fact that he was apparently before the highest court awaiting a final verdict, point to Rome as the place.

Although Paul was a prisoner, he was allowed to live in a rented residence as he awaited the outcome of his trial (Acts 28:30). He spent his time writing letters, teaching visitors, encouraging brethren, etc. Eventually, the court ruled in his favor and he was acquitted.

CITY OF PHILIPPI

Philippi was located in eastern Macedonia about 10 miles inland from the Aegean Sea. The original settlement was named Krenides, but the name was changed to Philippi when the father of Alexander the Great, Philip II of Macedon, took control of it.

Philippi had been the site of a decisive battle in which Antony and Octavian defeated Brutus and Cassius, the assassins of Julius Caesar (B.C. 42). Antony celebrated the victory by settling some of his veterans there and the city was made a Roman colony. Philippi became a "Rome away from Rome."

Philippi was a wealthy city, primarily because of its location along the Egnatian Way, which was the major east-west highway of the Roman Empire. The city was also famous for its school of medicine and agriculture.

Paul came to Philippi after he received "The Macedonian Call" (Acts 16:9-10). Macedonia was a Roman province and home to such cities as Philippi, Thessalonica, and Berea. Paul did not make the trip alone. He was accompanied by Luke, Silas, and Timothy.

CHURCH AT PHILIPPI

The church at Philippi was founded by Paul during his second missionary journey (A.D. 49-52). Acts 16 records his entrance into the city after receiving a vision in the night. When he arrived, he converted two households—the households of Lydia and the jailor.

It was Paul's custom to seek out the synagogue in each city he visited (Acts 13:5, 14; 14:1; 17:2, 10, 17; 18:4, 19; 19:8). However, Philippi apparently did not have a synagogue since he went to the riverside on the Sabbath. In cases where there was no synagogue in the city, Jewish worshippers often assembled near water in order to perform their ceremonial washings. That is where Paul met Lydia.

It is interesting to note that the first convert in Philippi was a woman from Thyatira in the province of Asia, which Paul had been prevented from entering before coming to Philippi. Having been forbidden to travel into Asia, the apostle went to Macedonia and converted a woman from Asia! Lydia was probably a widow since Luke referred to "her household" (Acts 16:15).

Although we do not know much about the members of the Philippian church, we can compile a short list of individual members: Lydia, the jailor, Epaphroditus, Euodia, Syntyche, and Clement. It is likely that Luke was a member of the Philippian congregation, at least for a time, since he stayed in the city when Paul left for Thessalonica on his second journey (Acts 16:40) and was still there when Paul returned on his third journey (Acts 20:6).

The Philippian church was very generous. This noble characteristic started with the initial converts who showed Paul such great hospitality (Acts 16:15, 34) and continued during the 10 years that elapsed since that time (Philippians 1:5). They were not only generous to Paul, but also to needy brethren (2 Corinthians 8:1-4). Later, Polycarp commended the church for its hospitality.

LETTER TO PHILIPPI

The Philippian letter is one of the so-called "Prison Letters," that is, letters that were written during Paul's first Roman imprisonment. The others were Ephesians, Colossians, and Philemon. Those three letters were written at the same time and sent to the same area—the province of Asia. Philippians was written a short time later and sent to a different area—the province of Macedonia.

There were several reasons why Paul wrote to the Philippians.

(1) **To Thank.** The Philippians had sent a monetary gift to Paul by the hands of Epaphroditus, who was to stay with the apostle as an assistant. Paul wrote to express his thankfulness for their generosity (1:3-5; 4:10, 14-18).

(2) **To Commend.** The Philippians had planned for Epaphroditus to stay with the apostle for an extended period of time. However, Paul was sending him back early. Paul wrote to commend Epaphroditus to the Philippians for a job well done (2:25-30).

(3) **To Encourage.** The Philippians were suffering the same type of persecution that the apostle had suffered in the city. Paul wrote to encourage them to remain steadfast (1:27-30).

(4) **To Unite.** There was disunity in the congregation at Philippi. Paul wrote to urge unity among the members (2:14; 4:2).

(5) **To Warn.** Judaizers were Jewish Christians who tried to bind parts of the Old Law on brethren. They plagued many of the early churches. Paul wrote to warn the Philippians about Judaizers (3:2, 18-19).

Paul sent the letter to the Philippians by the hands of Epaphroditus. Polycarp said that Paul wrote "letters" to the congregation, which is not surprising when we consider how fond Paul was of the brethren there. Paul wrote several letters to churches that are not recorded in scripture (see 1 Corinthians 5:9; Colossians 4:16).

CHAPTER ONE

SALUTING

<u></u>

(vv. 1-2)

1) Paul and Timothy, servants of Christ Jesus, To all the saints in Christ Jesus who are at Philippi, with the overseers and deacons.

Paul was the founder of the church at Philippi and an apostle of Jesus Christ. Following the customary style of letters in the first century (writer--recipients--salutation--message--final greeting), Paul identified himself as the writer. **Timothy** was a young preacher and close companion of Paul. He was with the apostle when the church at Philippi was established and at the time of this writing. For a detailed study of Timothy, see notes at 2:19. Since Paul used first-person singular throughout the letter and since Timothy is referred to in the third person in 2:19, we should not take the inclusion of Timothy's name to mean that he was an equal co-writer. Rather, he is identified as a co-worker and possibly the one who penned the words for Paul. Timothy is mentioned with Paul in the opening greeting of six letters (2 Corinthians 1:1; Philippians 1:1; Colossians 1:1; 1 Thessalonians 1:1; 2 Thessalonians 1:1; Philemon 1). **Servants** is better translated as slaves. They had been bought with a price (1 Corinthians 7:23). This designation emphasizes both submission to and dependence on the Lord. Other writers of the New Testament also referred to themselves as slaves. Interestingly, the same term is used in 2:7 of Christ. This is one of the few letters in which Paul omitted calling himself an apostle. The others are 1 Thessalonians, 2 Thessalonians, and Philemon. There was no need for Paul to identify himself as an apostle because no one in the congregation questioned his authority.

> When not necessary to vindicate his teaching as from God, he was modest and unassuming and placed himself on an equality with the humblest servant of the Lord Jesus Christ. He assumed no titles or dignities. (2)

Christ means anointed one. It is equivalent to the Hebrew "Messiah." **Jesus** is the personal name of Christ, and means Yahweh saves. It is equivalent to the Hebrew "Joshua." "Christ" appears 37 times in the letter, 18 times in the first chapter, and "Jesus" appears 22 times total. **All** is a significant word in the letter (1:1, 4, 7, 8, 25; 2:17, 26; 4:21). It emphasizes togetherness; none were excluded. This is a subtle way to promote a spirit of unity (1:27; 2:1-4; 4:2-3). **Saints** are those who have been set apart or sanctified; they are God's holy people. All Christians are saints. One becomes a saint through baptism (Ephesians 5:26). This term appears three times in the letter (1:1; 4:21, 22). **In Christ** refers to their spiritual state. We are baptized into Christ (Romans 6:3; Galatians 3:27). **Philippi** was a city of Macedonia where the saints to whom Paul wrote lived. **Overseers** are men who superintend the local church. Overseers are often called elders (Acts 20:17, 28; Titus 1:5, 7). In the New Testament, each congregation had a plurality of elders (Acts 14:23; 15:4; 20:17; Philippians 1:1; 1 Thessalonians 5:12; James 5:14). Elders must meet certain qualifications (1 Timothy 3:1-7; Titus 1:5-9). **Deacons** means servants. The term is used in both a general and technical sense. It is used in a technical sense in this text, referring to a special group of servants who tend to the physical needs of the local church. Like elders, deacons must meet certain qualifications (1 Timothy 3:8-13). Deacons are probably listed second because they are subject to the elders. In no other letter does Paul mention elders and deacons in the greeting.

The qualifications for an elder and deacon exclude women from serving in those capacities. For instance, only men are the husband of one wife (1 Timothy 3:2, 12). That fact was apparently ignored when certain English translators chose to call Phoebe a deacon (NRSV) rather than servant. The Greek word *diakonon* was used in a general sense in that passage, and was not referring to a church officer.

2) Grace to you and peace from God our Father and the Lord Jesus Christ.

Grace means unmerited favor. **Peace** is the result of grace, and refers to the inner calmness that comes from being reconciled to God. It is tranquility even in the midst of turmoil. It is from this Greek word *(eirene)* that we get our English word "serene." **God our Father** is the first person of the Godhead. This description points to His authority and provision for those who belong to Him. **Lord** is used 15 times in the letter, and denotes supreme authority. Though the Roman emperor assumed this title for himself, there is but one true Lord (1 Corinthians 8:6). **Jesus Christ** is the second person of the Godhead (see v. 1). This salutation was commonly employed by Paul in the New Testament.

SHARING

(vv. 3-11)

3) I thank my God in all my remembrance of you.

Paul had fond memories of the Philippians and was thankful for them. **I** is first-person singular, which shows that the inclusion of Timothy's name in verse 1 did not mean that he was an equal co-writer. He has already faded into the background. **Thank** is in the present tense, and denotes continual gratitude. It is from this Greek word *(eucharisto)* that we get our English word "Eucharist." **My** emphasizes the personal relationship that Paul shared with God (4:19; Romans 1:8; 1 Corinthians 1:4; 2 Corinthians 12:21; Philemon 4). Although Paul had been severely mistreated in Philippi (1 Thessalonians 2:2), his mind was full of good memories of the church there. When he thinks, he thanks! "My remembrance…my heart…my prayer" (vv. 3, 7, 9).

4) Always in every prayer of mine for you all making my prayer with joy.

Paul was a man of prayer. He often prayed for the churches and solicited their prayers in return. **Always** indicates the frequency with which Paul offered thanks in prayer. Such language is common in the letters of Paul (Romans 1:10; 1 Corinthians 1:4; Ephesians 5:20; Colossians 1:3; 1 Thessalonians 1:2; 2 Thessalonians 1:3, 11; 2:13; Philemon 4). **All** includes every member. **Joy** is a significant word in this letter (1:4, 18, 25; 2:2, 17, 18, 28, 29; 3:1; 4:1, 4, 10). It is no wonder that Philippians is often called

"The Letter of Joy." It was a joy for Paul to pray for the brethren in Philippi.

5) Because of your partnership in the gospel from the first day until now.

Paul now explained the reasons for his joy. One reason was short term (immediate) and the other was long term (ultimate). First, they had been consistent partners in the gospel. **Partnership** refers to joint-participation or sharing. This Greek word *(koinonia)* was a favorite word of Paul, and was often used of monetary contributions (Acts 2:42; Romans 15:26; 2 Corinthians 8:4; 9:13; Hebrews 13:16). That is the idea here. The Philippians partnered with Paul in financial support (4:15). They had sent money to Paul in Thessalonica (Philippians 4:16), in Corinth (2 Corinthians 11:9), and in Rome (Philippians 4:10, 18). Refreshingly, there is no hint that this partnership was ever marred by suspicion as in other places. **The gospel** appears several times in the letter (1:5, 7, 12, 16, 27; 2:2; 4:3, 15) and refers to the entire body of truth. The gospel is to be obeyed (Romans 10:16; 2 Thessalonians 1:8; 1 Peter 4:17). It has inherent power to save sinners (Romans 1:16) and will be the standard of judgment (Romans 2:16). **From the first day** refers to the time when Paul came to Philippi on his second missionary journey. **Until now** refers to Paul's current imprisonment in Rome.

6) And I am sure of this, that he who began a good work in you will bring it to completion at the day of Jesus Christ.

The second reason for Paul's joy was his confidence that God would bring the good work He began among the Philippians to completion. God will finish what He started! **I am sure** denotes confidence or trust. This Greek word *(pepoithos)* is used six times in the letter (1:6, 14, 25; 2:24; 3:3, 4). **He who began** is God. **A good work** refers to their conversion and growth in Christ, which was evidenced by their partnership with Paul in the gospel. This is a great example of the apostle's humility. He readily acknowledged that it was God, and not himself, who began a good work in the Philippians. Paul firmly believed that God was active in their lives (2:13). **The day of Jesus Christ** is the Second Coming (v. 10; 2:16). The Second Coming is called "the day of wrath" (Romans 2:5), "the day of redemption" (Ephesians 4:30), "the day of judgment" (2 Peter 3:7), etc. Paul always had his eyes focused on "that Day" (2 Timothy 4:8).

Calvinists misuse this text to support the notion that it is impossible for a saved person to ultimately be lost. This doctrine is often called the "perseverance of the saints." However, they still had to work out their own salvation with fear and trembling (2:12) and guard against those who could lead them astray (3:2, 18-19).

7) It is right for me to feel this way about you all, because I hold you in my heart, for you are all partakers with me of grace, both in my imprisonment and in the defense and confirmation of the gospel.

Paul had strong feelings for the Philippians. **It is right** means morally acceptable. This is reminiscent of 2 Thessalonians 1:3, which says "as is right." **This way** refers to his thankfulness (v. 3), joy (v. 4), and surety (v. 6). **All** includes every member. **I hold you in my heart** is reminiscent of 2 Corinthians 7:3, which says "you are in our hearts." Due to ambiguity in the Greek text, it is possible that Paul meant to say "because you hold me in such affection" (NEB).

> There is no way to decide which is the idea meant
> except to say that love begets love. (3)

Grace is preceded by the definite article ("the") in the Greek text. Therefore, Paul may have reference to the plan of grace, that is, the body of truth. The more likely meaning, however, is that God granted them the favor of sharing with Paul in his afflictions (see 3:10). **Partakers** means they share with. **Imprisonment** appears four times in this letter, all in the first chapter (1:7, 13, 14, 17). The NIV says "in chains." Paul was chained to a guard in a rented residence. The length of the chain was 18 inches. The prisoner's right wrist was chained to the guard's left wrist, which gave the guard an upper hand if an altercation occurred. **Defense** is a legal term, and refers to a verbal answer. It is from this Greek word *(apologia)* that we get our English word "apologetics." **Confirmation** means to establish. Paul both defended (negative) and confirmed (positive) the gospel. The Philippians were partakers of Paul's chains, defense, and confirmation by their support. Similarly, 3 John 8 says that those who assist preachers are fellow workers for the truth.

8) For God is my witness, how I yearn for you all with the affection of Christ Jesus.

For God is my witness is a solemn affirmation (Romans 1:9; 2 Corinthians 1:23; Galatians 1:20; 1 Thessalonians 2:5, 10). Only God could know Paul's innermost feelings about the Philippians. This was said to emphasize the truthfulness of his words; there was no exaggeration or hyperbole. **Yearn for** denotes strong desire; to long for (2:26; 4:1; Romans 1:11; 1 Thessalonians 3:6; 2 Timothy 1:4). **All** includes every member. **Affection** is from a Greek word *(splanchnois)* that refers to internal organs ("bowels," KJV). However, with the exception of Acts 1:18, the word is used metaphorically in the New Testament to denote the center of affection.

> This verse provides one of the best examples of the fact that a literal translation may actually be an incorrect translation. Paul says that he longs after the Philippians in the "bowels" of Jesus Christ...The Greeks thought of the bowels as the center of affection. But we use the term "heart" for that. So the translation "bowels" here is actually misleading. Not only does it convey entirely the wrong idea, but it is apt to start the mind off on a sidetrack of unpleasant thought that will divert attention away from the true meaning of the passage. (4)

Paul loved the Philippians in the same way that Jesus loved them. The CEV says "I care for you in the same way that Christ Jesus does." Although Paul was far away and had not seen them for some time, his love for them was still burning intensely. Only in Christ would a Jewish man have felt so warmly for former pagans!

Paul expressed his prayer for the Philippian church. Verses 5-8 could be viewed as parenthetical, with verse 9 picking up the reference to prayer in verse 4.

9) And it is my prayer that your love may abound more and more, with knowledge and all discernment.

Paul prayed for their continued spiritual progress. **Love** is from a Greek word *(agape)* that refers to love that goes beyond emotion and seeks the very best for its object. It is a sacrificial and selfless love. It loves the unlovable! **Abound** means to overflow. It denotes continual increase. **More and more** is added for emphasis. This is reminiscent of 1 Thessalonians 3:12, which says "may the Lord make you increase and abound in love for one another and for all." **Knowledge** refers to a comprehensive knowledge of truth. **Discernment** refers to the ability to discern between right and wrong; sensitive moral perception. Knowledge and discernment are inseparably linked to love.

Agape is described in detail in 1 Corinthians 13:4-8. It is used in passages that speak of God's love for the world (John 3:16) and man's love for his wife (Ephesians 5:25), his neighbor (Romans 13:9), and his enemies (Matthew 5:44). *Agape* is a fruit of the Spirit (Galatians 5:22). This kind of love would end the dispute between the squabbling sisters (see 4:2).

10) So that you may approve what is excellent, and so be pure and blameless for the day of Christ.

So that links this verse to the one before. Love coupled with knowledge and discernment would allow the Philippians to approve what is excellent, which would result in purity and blamelessness for the day of Christ. **Approve** means to determine by testing. This Greek word *(dokimazein)* is used of a person's self-examination before eating the Lord Supper (1 Corinthians 11:28). **Excellent** refers to that which is of priority. The NIV says "what is best." **Pure** denotes one who is genuine; unsullied. The NASB says "sincere." **Blameless** means without stumbling or offense. **The day of Christ** is the Second Coming (v. 6; 2:16).

11) Filled with the fruit of righteousness that comes through Jesus Christ, to the glory and praise of God.

The fruit of righteousness is fruit that is produced by righteousness. It is the good which righteousness prompts its possessor to do. This fruit is called "the fruit of the Spirit" in Galatians 5:22, and includes love, joy, peace, patience, kindness, goodness, faithfulness, gentleness, and self-control. This same phrase appears in James 3:18, where the word is translated "harvest." **That comes through Jesus Christ** identifies Christ as the source (John 15:1-10).

> The fruit comes through Jesus Christ. Personal effort is involved, even as effort is involved in producing physical fruit; but the ultimate source of both physical and spiritual fruit is the Lord. One writer pointed out

that a tree or vine does not make a lot of noise while it produces fruit. When someone understands that it is *the Lord* who is the source of "fruit" in our lives, this should eliminate pride and self-promotion. (5)

To the glory and praise of God was the ultimate objective for their actions. All that we do as Christians should be to God's glory (Matthew 5:16; 1 Corinthians 10:31; 1 Peter 4:11).

SPREADING

(vv. 12-18)

Paul moved into the body of the letter at this point. This section can be divided into two parts: gospel unchained (vv. 12-14) and focus unchained (vv. 15-18). Paul wanted to inform the brethren of his circumstances in Roman confinement in order to relieve anxiety and increase steadfastness. The gospel had not been suppressed but progressed! It was spreading in ways that it had not spread before.

This section can also be more broadly divided into three parts: Paul's chains (vv. 12-14), Paul's critics (vv. 15-18), and Paul's crisis (vv. 19-26).

12) I want you to know, brothers, that what has happened to me has really served to advance the gospel.

I want you to know is a common expression in Paul's writings (Romans 1:13; 11:25; 1 Corinthians 10:1; 12:1; 2 Corinthians 1:8; 1 Thessalonians 4:13), and expresses his desire that they be informed of something important. **Brothers** is an affectionate term that denotes their spiritual kinship. They were adopted into the family of God with Christ as their older brother. This term of endearment is used nine times in the letter (1:12, 14; 2:25; 3:1, 13, 17; 4:1, 8, 21), and often appears at the beginning of a new paragraph. This Greek word *(adelphoi)* refers to all believers, both men and women. The NIV says "brothers and sisters." A parallel expression is "my beloved" (2:12; 4:1). **What has happened to me** refers to the circumstances of his imprisonment. **Has served to advance the gospel** means that the gospel was being progressed. Paul's confinement may have bound the messenger but not the message (see 2 Timothy 2:9). The same God who used Moses' rod and David's sling was using Paul's chains to spread the gospel! The saints in Jerusalem being scattered (Acts 8) and Paul and Barnabas separating before the second missionary journey (Acts 15) are other instances in which seemingly bad situations resulted in the advancement of the gospel.

"Providence" is the working of God in advance to arrange circumstances and situations for the fulfilling of His purposes. Throughout scripture, God worked in the lives of men and women providentially to bring about certain outcomes (Joseph, Ruth, Esther, Onesimus, etc).

In verses 13-14, Paul gave two examples of how his imprisonment served to spread the gospel. The first example pertained to unbelievers while the second example pertained to believers.

13) So that it has become known throughout the whole imperial guard and to all the rest that my imprisonment is for Christ.

The first example of how the gospel was advanced by Paul's imprisonment pertained to unbelievers--they were exposed to the truth. **Known** means clearly visible. **The imperial guard** was an elite group of Roman soldiers. As an imperial prisoner, Paul was always chained to a member of the guard. Shifts usually rotated every six hours, which means that Paul influenced up to four guards per day. (Some suggest shifts changed every four hours, which would increase the number to six per day)! As the guards heard Paul talk about the gospel and observed his manner of living, they learned of Christ and the apostle's work of proclaiming Him. In other words, they came to realize that Paul was "a prisoner for Christ Jesus" (Ephesians 3:1; Philemon 1).

> The guards relieved each other. In this way ever so many of them came into contact with this apostle to the Gentiles. They took note of his patience, gentleness, courage, and unswerving loyalty to inner conviction. They were deeply impressed. Yes, even these hardened soldiers, these rude legionaries, who presumably would be the very last to be affected in any way by the gospel, were deeply moved by what they saw and heard and felt in the presence of Paul. They listened to him as he talked to friends who came to visit him, or to his secretary to whom he dictated his letters, or to his judges, or to God in prayer, or even to themselves…And what they learned they began to spread. (6)

All the rest refers to other unbelievers who either visited with or heard about Paul (see 4:22). Onesimus was an unbeliever who was influenced by the apostle during his imprisonment (Philemon 10-16). This could also refer to various court officials who had come in contact with the apostle up to this point. **Is for Christ** means for the cause of Christ, as opposed to some political motivation or crime committed. Paul was not motivated by insurrection but resurrection!

Who was chained to whom? Since Paul had appealed to Caesar (Acts 25:11), he was placed in the care of the imperial guard. Though in a rented residence (Acts 28:30), he was bound to a member of the guard. Hence, the guards could not help but to hear the message and observe the apostle's conduct. In that sense, they were a captive audience!

> If Paul had gone to Rome as originally planned, and had preached in the Roman forum, probably not one of the soldiers would have stopped to listen to him. However, since they were chained to him night and day, he would have been hard to ignore. (7)

14) And most of the brothers, having become confident in the Lord by my imprisonment, are much more bold to speak the word without fear.

The second example of how the gospel was advanced by Paul's imprisonment pertained to believers--they were emboldened to speak the truth. **Most** not all. **The brothers** were Christians living in Rome. There was already a rather large number of Christians in Rome when Paul arrived there. When they saw how he trusted in the Lord and maintained his joy in spite of the circumstances, they grew more confident. Courage is contagious! **In the Lord** is the sphere of their confidence. **Bold** means daring. **Speak** is from a Greek word *(lalein)* that refers to general communication. Therefore, many believe that Paul had personal evangelism in mind rather than public addresses. **The word** is the gospel (see 1:5). **Without fear** of consequences. They were not intimidated but invigorated! "Confident…much more bold… without fear."

Though many of the Christians in Rome were commendable, there were some preachers who had impure motives. They preached the truth out of rivalry. The problem was not the message but the messenger.

15) Some indeed preach Christ from envy and rivalry, but others from good will.

There were two groups of preachers in Rome. Although both groups taught the truth, their motives were different. The contrast between the two groups is clear: good will/envy and rivalry (v. 15), love/rivalry (vv. 16-17), knowing/thinking (vv. 16-17), truth/pretense (v. 18). **Some** refers to the group with impure motives. **Preach Christ** indicates that they were teaching the truth. **Envy** is resentment at the success of others. **Rivalry** is selfish ambition. These two vices are listed among the works of the flesh (Galatians 5:20-21). The group with impure motives apparently viewed Paul as a threat to their own prestige. They had the spirit of Diotrophes (3 John 9-10). **Others** refers to the group with pure motives. **Good will** is an attitude that seeks the best for others. This parallels "out of love" (v. 16) and "in truth" (v. 18).

16) The latter do it out of love, knowing that I am put here for the defense of the gospel.

Following the Textus Receptus, the King James Version (KJV) reverses the order of verses 16 and 17. **The latter** is the group with pure motives. **Love** is from a Greek word *(agape)* that refers to love that goes beyond emotion and seeks the very best for its object (see v. 9). This group appreciated the fact that Paul was suffering for the sake of the gospel. **Put here** denotes divine appointment. This Greek word *(keimai)* is translated "destined" in 1 Thessalonians 3:3. God had providentially brought Paul to this point. **Defense** refers to a verbal answer (see v. 7).

17) The former proclaim Christ out of rivalry, not sincerely but thinking to afflict me in my imprisonment.

Imprisonment was not Paul's only burden. He had to bear the pain of certain brethren who tried to afflict him. **The former** is the group with impure motives. **Proclaim Christ** indicates that they were teaching the truth. **Rivalry** is selfish ambition. **Afflict** means to distress. Obviously, it does not refer to physical affliction since Paul was being safely guarded. It refers to inner turmoil.

The rival preachers assumed that their evangelistic successes would make Paul jealous, increasing the burden of his confinement and making his life more miserable. (8)

These men were condemned by the very message they proclaimed. This should serve as a warning to all preachers!

18) What then? Only that in every way, whether in pretense or in truth, Christ is proclaimed, and in that I rejoice. Yes, and I will rejoice.

The NRSV says "What does it matter?" Paul was not concerned with his own welfare. So long as the truth was proclaimed, he had reason to rejoice. This is a shining example of Paul's humility. His personal feelings, comfort, and reputation were unimportant. He was not concerned with what they were doing *to* him, but with what they were doing *for* the gospel. He was rejoicing, not retaliating! **Whether...or** denotes contrasting options. This combined conjunction appears three times in the first chapter (vv. 18, 20, 27). **Pretense** refers to false motives. This Greek word *(prophasei)* is translated "pretext" in 1 Thessalonians 2:5. **Truth** is the opposite of pretense in this text, and refers to true motives. They were transparent. **Christ is proclaimed** indicates that truth was being taught. Even if some had false motives, Paul could at least rejoice that the message was being spread.

Paul would not have been nearly as reserved if truth were at stake. To suggest that this same spirit should prevail when dealing with false teachers is an abuse of the text.

> There is no evidence whatever that these rivals of Paul were teaching religious *error* (as do modern sectarians)...only their base motives and selfish ambitions come under the apostle's critical pen. This context is no shelter for the protection of those who would teach doctrines that are subversive to the gospel of Christ, and it is wrong to pervert it to such an end. (9)

Since both groups were teaching the truth, the Judaizers mentioned later in the letter must be excluded from consideration. They preached "a different gospel" (Galatians 1:6). Paul would not rejoice in any aspect of what they were doing.

SPARING

(vv. 19-26)

Having mentioned the circumstances of his confinement in Rome, Paul pondered the possible outcome of his trial. His case had reached the high court. The verdict would be final. He knew that his life was at stake, and contemplated which outcome he preferred. There is an obvious progression of thought in this section, and one can easily sense the apostle's assurance of eternal life regardless of his trial's outcome. He finally determined that his life would be spared for their sakes.

19) For I know that through your prayers and the help of the Spirit of Jesus Christ this will turn out for my deliverance.

Paul found reason to rejoice in the expectation of deliverance. This would be accomplished by God through their prayers and the help of the Spirit of Jesus Christ. **Know** refers to confident knowledge. **Through your prayers** reveals how strongly Paul felt about the power of prayer. He firmly believed that their prayers could impact his future. This is reminiscent of Philemon 22, which says "through your prayers I will be graciously given to you." **Help** denotes bountiful supply for what is needed. It is from this Greek word *(epichoregias)* that we get our English word "chorus."

> Whenever a Greek city was going to put on a special festival, somebody had to pay for the singers and dancers. The donation called for had to be a lavish one, and so this word came to mean "to provide generously and lavishly." (10)

The Spirit of Jesus Christ is the Holy Spirit. He is called the Spirit of Jesus Christ because of His close relationship with the Lord. Paul fully anticipated that the Spirit would supply his needs before the court. This probably refers to the actual words that Paul would speak (see Matthew 10:19-20). **Deliverance** from prison. This Greek word *(soterian)* was also used of eternal salvation in the letter (1:28; 2:12).

20) As it is my eager expectation and hope that I will not be at all ashamed, but that with full courage now as always Christ will be honored in my body, whether by life or by death.

In addition to being confident about his release, Paul was confident that he would honor Christ as he had done before. **Eager expectation and hope** are aspects of a single concept. The words are used synonymously, and refer to confident anticipation. **That I will not be at all ashamed** refers to his trial. Paul did not want to do or say anything that would bring reproach upon Christ. **Full courage** refers to unreservedness of utterance. The NRSV says "with all boldness." **Honored** means magnified. The NEB says "the greatness of Christ will shine out clearly." **Whether by life or by death** means regardless of the outcome. Paul wanted to honor Christ whether he was acquitted or executed.

21) For to me to live is Christ, and to die is gain.

This verse summed up Paul's perspective on life and death. **To live is Christ** means that Christ animated and permeated every fiber of Paul's being (Romans 14:8; Galatians 2:20; Colossians 3:4). Paul was not self-centered but Christ-centered! **To die is gain** means that death, which is separation of the soul from the body (James 2:26), has certain advantages for the apostle. He would be free from the trials and tribulations of this life and be in closer relation to the Lord.

22) If I am to live in the flesh, that means fruitful labor for me. Yet which I shall choose I cannot tell.

One can sense an internal struggle within the mind of Paul. If it were his choice to make, which outcome would he prefer? **Flesh** means body. **Fruitful labor** refers to work in the gospel that results in souls saved and saints edified. If Paul were to be acquitted, he would continue reaping fruit for the Lord.

> If he should continue to live as a result of a favorable disposition of his case in Rome, this would provide continued opportunity for him to labor fruitfully in the cause of Christ. For Paul this never meant an easy life. His labors in establishing churches and nurturing them toward maturity were characterized by frequent opposition, physical hardships, and much spiritual anguish. Yet he looked on his apostolic ministry as a challenge to be grasped and as fruit to be harvested. (11)

Yet which I shall choose I cannot tell does not mean that the choice was Paul's to make. The apostle merely pondered which outcome he would prefer.

23) I am hard pressed between the two. My desire is to depart and be with Christ, for that is far better.

Hard pressed means hemmed in on both sides. This Greek word (*synechomai*) is used of a pressing crowd in Luke 8:45 and of a military entrapment in Luke 19:43. Paul finally determined his preference. **Depart** means to unloose. It refers to physical death (2 Timothy 4:6). **And be with Christ** has caused some confusion since departed spirits abide in Hades until the Judgment (Luke 16:19-31; Revelation 20:13). There are two possible explanations: (1) Paul anticipated being with the Lord in a fuller sense in Hades. (2) Paul anticipated being with the Lord ultimately in heaven. If this is so, Paul passed over the time between death and the resurrection (see Hebrews 9:27). **Far better** means that it is better to depart and be with the Lord than to remain in the flesh.

Hades is equivalent to the Hebrew "Sheol," and means unseen. It refers to the abode of the dead. Hades is the realm where all disembodied spirits abide until the Second Coming of Christ. The spirit of Jesus went to Hades at death (Acts 2:27, 31). Hades is divided into two parts; one is a place of comfort and one is a place of torment (Luke 16:19-31). The former is called "paradise" (Luke 23:43) and the latter is called "prison" (1 Peter 3:19). Hades will be destroyed when the Lord returns for final judgment (Revelation 20:14). Jesus is the ruler of Hades (Revelation 1:18).

24) But to remain in the flesh is more necessary on your account.

Death would be "far better" but living was "more necessary." **Necessary** or needful. Although the Philippian church was impressive in many ways, it still had its share of problems (3:1-3, 19; 4:2). Therefore, Paul concluded that it was more necessary to remain for their sakes. Paul put their interests above his own (2:3-4).

25) Convinced of this, I know that I will remain and continue with you all, for your progress and joy in the faith.

Convinced denotes confidence or trust (see 1:6). Paul was confident that the Lord would let him live for their sakes. **I know** refers to personal conviction in this text. Paul had not received a direct revelation about his outcome (2:17, 23-24). In Acts 20:25, Paul used this same Greek word *(oida)* when he told the Ephesian elders that they would not see him again, yet they did see him again. **Progress** denotes spiritual advancement. **All** is every member. **Joy** is a keynote of the letter, and goes hand in hand with spiritual advancement. **The faith** is the body of truth. There is evidence that Paul was released from this imprisonment and traveled back to Macedonia.

26) So that in me you may have ample cause to glory in Christ Jesus, because of my coming to you again.

If Paul were acquitted and able to return in person to Philippi, they would have ample reason to rejoice in the Lord. **Glory** means boast. This Greek word *(kauchema)* is translated "proud" in 2:16. **In Christ Jesus** is the sphere of glorying.

STANDING

(vv. 27-30)

At this point, the focus shifted from Paul's affairs to their affairs. The Philippians were instructed on matters internal and external. There are three main points: stand together (v. 27), strive together (v. 27), and suffer together (v. 29).

27) Only let your manner of life be worthy of the gospel of Christ, so that whether I come and see you or am absent, I may hear of you that you are standing firm in one spirit, with one mind striving side by side for the faith of the gospel.

Only is emphatic in Greek, and indicates the importance of what Paul is about to say. The TEV says "Now, the important thing." **Manner of life** refers to conduct or behavior. Christians are obligated to conduct themselves in a manner that is worthy of the gospel. This Greek word *(politeuesthe)* means to be a citizen, which would have obvious significance to the Philippians.

> The exhortation contemplates the Philippians as members of the Christian commonwealth. The figure would be naturally suggested to Paul by his residence in Rome, and would appeal to the Philippians as a Roman colony, which was a reproduction of the parent commonwealth on a smaller scale. (12)

Christians are to live in a manner worthy "of the calling" (Ephesians 4:1), "of the Lord" (Colossians 1:10), "of God" (1 Thessalonians 2:12), etc. **Whether I come and see you** anticipates his acquittal, release, and return to Philippi. **Or am absent** contemplates an unfavorable outcome in which he is restrained from returning to Philippi. Either way, Paul urged the brethren to live right. The "come or absent" theme appears again in 2:12.

Standing firm denotes steadfast persistence (also 4:1). Paul often called on congregations to stand firm (1 Corinthians 16:13; Galatians 5:1; Ephesians 6:13; 2 Thessalonians 2:15). He wanted them to hold their ground. **One spirit, with one mind** are aspects of a single concept, and refer to a unified disposition. **Striving side by side** denotes joint-contending, as in an athletic contest. The NIV says "striving together as one." **The faith of the gospel** is the body of truth. Although unity is always needed, it is all the more necessary during times of intense persecution (vv. 28-30).

Jesus said that "every kingdom divided against itself is laid waste, and no city or house divided against itself will stand" (Matthew 12:25). Therefore, it is imperative that Christians be "united in the same mind and the same judgment" (1 Corinthians 1:10). Throughout this letter Paul pleaded for unity (1:27; 2:1-2; 4:2-3).

28) And not frightened in anything by your opponents. This is a clear sign to them of their destruction, but of your salvation, and that from God.

Christianity is not a passive religion. We are in a spiritual warfare and need to "fight the good fight of the faith" (1 Timothy 6:12). The Philippians had many foes, which included unbelievers and erring brethren. **Frightened** means terrified or startled. The word was used for spooked horses. **Opponents** are adversaries of the gospel. Paul did not want them to be intimidated in the least by their opponents. **Sign** means proof. **Destruction** refers to eternal damnation. **Salvation** refers to eternal life. Their courage was evidence that their opponents were doomed and they were saved.

Whom to fear? Christians in the first century had many opponents. However, they were not to fear what men could do. Jesus said, "Do not fear those who kill the body but cannot kill the soul. Rather fear him who can destroy both soul and body in hell" (Matthew 10:28).

29) For it has been granted to you that for the sake of Christ you should not only believe in him but also suffer for his sake.

Paul already said that it was a favor to partake in his sufferings (v. 7). Now he said that it was a favor to suffer for Christ. **Granted** is from the same root word as grace. There were two graces bestowed on the Philippians according to this verse: belief and suffering. Belief had been granted to them just as repentance had been granted to the Gentiles in Acts 11:18, that is, through providential circumstances. The fact that both belief and repentance are commanded in scripture proves that man has a part. **Suffer** refers to external persecution. **For his sake** qualifies the suffering of which he spoke (see 1 Peter 4:15-16). Jesus said that those who suffer for Him are "blessed" (Matthew 5:10-12). To suffer for Christ is a gift of grace.

Paul said that "all who desire to live a godly life in Christ Jesus will be persecuted" (2 Timothy 3:12). Early Christians suffered assault, exile, expulsion, imprisonment, property-confiscation, and even death. However, they were to view such suffering as a grace, not a disgrace! The Macedonian churches, which included Philippi, were under constant distress (2 Corinthians 8:2).

Calvinists misuse this text to support the notion that man is incapable of believing on his own. They say that faith must be supernaturally bestowed by God. However, the Philippians were given faith in the same sense in which they were given suffering, that is, through providential circumstances. God no more gave them faith supernaturally than He gave them suffering supernaturally.

30) Engaged in the same conflict that you saw I had and now hear that I still have.

Conflict denotes great strain. It is from this Greek word *(agona)* that we get our English word "agony." The same word is used of the Lord's agony in the garden of Gethsemane (Luke 22:44). **You saw I had** refers to his sufferings in Philippi 10 years earlier (Acts 16; also 1 Thessalonians 2:2). **Now hear that I still have** refers to his sufferings in Rome. Paul reminded the Philippians that they were not alone in their struggles. He too had suffered and continued to suffer for Christ. In 1 Thessalonians 2:14-16, Paul encouraged the Thessalonians by appealing to the example of the Judean churches.

CHAPTER TWO

SUBMITTING

(vv. 1-11)

The second chapter of Philippians contains one of the riches portraits of Christ in scripture (vv. 6-11). He was put forth as the prime and unparalleled example of humility whom the Philippians should imitate; the essence of selfless submission. The chapter also includes details about Timothy (vv. 19-24) and Epaphroditus (vv. 25-30).

Later in the letter, Paul named two sisters who were squabbling (4:2). These words were written, no doubt, with them in mind.

1) So if there is any encouragement in Christ, any comfort from love, any participation in the Spirit, any affection and sympathy.

Paul employed a rhetorical device to emphasize the importance of the topic at hand. **If** assumes a truth. The idea is "since" or "because." **Encouragement** or exhortation. This Greek word (*paraklesis*) is translated "appeal" in 1 Thessalonians 2:3. **Comfort** or consolation. These two words are used together in 1 Corinthians 14:3. **Participation** or sharing (see 1:5). The idea could be participation *with* the Spirit or participation *through* the Spirit. **Affection** or tenderness. **Sympathy** or compassion. Affection and sympathy are complementary expressions. Paul was saying that since these things are so, the Philippians should fulfill the request of the next verse.

2) Complete my joy by being of the same mind, having the same love, being in full accord and of one mind.

Although Paul already had joy (1:4), he urged them to bring his joy to completion by their unity. **Joy** is a keynote of the letter. The four requests of this verse correlate with the four attributes of the previous verse. **Complete** means to fill full. **Same mind** refers to mutual thinking. **Same love** refers to mutual feelings. **Full accord** refers to mutual affection. This Greek word *(sympsychoi)* literally means of one soul. **One mind** refers to mutual purpose. Paul's plea for unity was probably intended to combat the traces of disunity that existed within the congregation (see 4:2).

3) Do nothing from rivalry or conceit, but in humility count others more significant than yourselves.

Verses 3 and 4 follow a "not this…but that" pattern. Paul already mentioned the impure motives of some preachers in Rome (1:15-18). Now he cautioned the brethren against such motives. **Rivalry** is selfish ambition. **Conceit** is vain glory. The NCV says "pride." **Humility** is lowliness of mind. Paul conducted himself "with all humility" (Acts 20:19) and urged churches to conduct themselves "with all humility" (Ephesians 4:2). Earlier in the letter, Paul demonstrated his humility by describing himself as a slave (1:1) and by his attitude toward those trying to harm him (1:18). Interestingly, the ancient world did not see humility as a virtue. The Greeks and Romans prided themselves in being proud. **Count** means to regard. **More significant** means better. The idea is deserving first consideration. This mindset is in keeping with love, which "does not insist on its own way" (1 Corinthians 13:5). Paul did not say "as significant" but "more significant."

4) Let each of you look not only to his own interests, but also to the interests of others.

Look means to carefully observe. The same word is translated "keep your eyes on" in 3:17. It is not wrong to look out for one's own interests. Each of us has concerns which require attention and provision. Paul was saying not to look out for our own interests *exclusively*. He urged the Philippians to be unselfish and considerate. Paul frequently called upon brethren to be concerned for others (see Ephesians 4:28-29). This attitude of selfless humility was the very opposite of Paul's opponents (v. 21).

Paul used Christ as the prime and unparalleled example of humility. Though in the form of God, Christ did not count equality with God a thing to be grasped, made himself nothing, took the form of a servant, was born in the likeness of men, and became obedient to the point of death on a cross. Christ did not demand His own rights, but gave them up for the good of others. Although Christians could not possibly match the example of Christ, they should strive to imitate it to the best of their abilities. This section can be divided into two parts: Christ's humiliation (vv. 5-8) and Christ's exaltation (vv. 9-11).

50

5) Have this mind among yourselves, which is yours in Christ Jesus.

Have this mind is present tense, and denotes habitual thinking. **This** points back to what Paul had just said about humility. **Mind** refers to disposition. **In Christ Jesus** is the sphere of humility. The alternate translation, "which was also in Christ Jesus," sets forth Christ as the example of humility.

6) Who, though he was in the form of God, did not count equality with God a thing to be grasped.

Many believe that verses 6-11 were an early hymn. **Who** is Jesus. **He was in the form of God** denotes preexistence. Jesus lived prior to the incarnation (John 1:1-3, 14). **Form** is from a Greek word *(morphe)* that often refers to the nature or essence of a thing. However, the word was also used of outward appearance.

> The word appears in ancient literature in reference to one's outward appearance--especially concerning the Greek gods. Further, the word only occurs a few times in the Septuagint where it usually refers to outward appearance (Jud. 8:18; Job 4:16; Is. 44:13; Dan. 5:6, 9-10; 7:28). Further still, beyond 2:6-7 the term *morphe* only appears in Mark 16:12 in the New Testament. In that verse it refers to another "form" or "outward appearance" taken by Jesus after the Resurrection. (13)

If *morphe* is used of outward appearance, then Paul referred to the external expression of the pre-incarnate Christ's inward nature, that is, the divine glory He shared with the Father in eternity (John 17:5). **Equality with God** means that Jesus was on equal-footing with the Father in eternity. This affirms the deity of Christ. **Grasped** means clung to or hoarded. Rather than grasping what rightfully belonged to Him, Jesus willingly relinquished the equality He shared with the Father for the sake of others (v. 4). To a much lesser degree, Moses relinquished his exalted position in Egypt for others (Hebrews 11:24-25).

7) But made himself nothing, taking the form of a servant, being born in the likeness of men.

Made himself indicates that the incarnation was a voluntary act. **Nothing** in relation to His former existence. Jesus gave up His divine glory and took on a subservient role to the Father. At no time, however, did Jesus ever give up His divine nature. **Servant** is the same Greek word used of Paul and Timothy in 1:1. The Master became a slave! **Born in the likeness of men** means that Jesus became flesh (John 1:14; 1 Timothy 3:16; Hebrews 2:14). In refuting those who said that flesh was inherently evil, John wrote, "By this you know the Spirit of God: every spirit that confesses that Jesus Christ has come in the flesh is from God, and every spirit that does not confess Jesus is not from God. This is the spirit of the antichrist, which you heard was coming and now is in the world already" (1 John 4:2-3).

8) And being found in human form, he humbled himself by becoming obedient to the point of death, even death on a cross.

Form is from a Greek word *(schemati)* that refers to outer appearance. It was sometimes used interchangeably with *morphe* among the Greeks. **Humbled himself** denotes voluntary action. Christ chose to lower Himself. **Becoming obedient** to the Father. **To the point of death, even death on a cross** emphasizes the degree of Christ's obedience. He was obedient to such an extent that He suffered the most brutal and torturous form of execution in the Roman empire--crucifixion!

> The suffering of death by crucifixion was intense, esp. in hot climates. Severe local inflammation, coupled with an insignificant bleeding of the jagged wounds, produced traumatic fever, which was aggravated by the exposure to the heat of the sun, the strained position of the body and insufferable thirst. The wounds swelled about the rough nails and the torn and lacerated tendons and nerves caused excruciating agony. The arteries of the head and stomach were surcharged with blood and a terrific throbbing headache ensued. The mind was confused and filled with anxiety and dread foreboding. The victim of crucifixion literally died a thousand deaths. Tetanus not rarely supervened and the rigors of the attending convulsions would tear at the wounds and add to the burden of pain, till at last the bodily forces were exhausted and the victim sank into unconsciousness and death. (14)

Crucifixion was so horrific that Roman citizens were exempt from it. The most degraded offenders of the empire (insurrectionists, murderers, slaves, etc.) were usually the subjects of crucifixion. Jesus lived as a slave and died as a slave! Constantine later abolished crucifixion out of respect for Christians.

Although the St. Andrew's cross (X) and the St. Anthony's cross (T) were used by the Romans, it is likely that the traditional Latin cross (†) was the one used at the Lord's crucifixion. We know that because the lengthy title "This is Jesus of Nazareth, the King of the Jews," which was written in three languages, was placed above His head.

The Jewish historian Josephus mentioned Christ's death on the cross in his writings.

> Now, there was about this time Jesus, a wise man, if it be lawful to call him a man, for he was a doer of wonderful works--a teacher of such men as receive the truth with pleasure. He drew over to him both many of the Jews, and many of the Gentiles. He was [the] Christ; and when Pilate, at the suggestion of the principal men amongst us, had condemned him to the cross, those that loved him at the first did not forsake him, for he appeared to them alive again the third day, as the divine prophets had foretold these and ten thousand other wonderful things concerning him; and the tribe of Christians, so named from him, are not extinct at this day. (15)

For the sake of others, Christ went from heaven to earth, from glory to shame, from Master to servant, and from life to death -- "even death on a cross!" The high cost of a free gift.

9) Therefore God has highly exalted him and bestowed on him the name that is above every name.

Humiliation led to exaltation. **God has highly exalted him** means that He raised Christ to a preeminent position. Jesus is frequently referred to as at the right hand of God (Acts 2:33; 5:31; 7:55-56; Romans 8:34; Ephesians 1:20; Colossians 3:1; Hebrews 1:3, 13; 8:1; 10:12; 12:2; 1 Peter 3:22). The resurrection and ascension are assumed in this text. Jesus had taught that those who humble themselves would be exalted (Matthew 23:12). **Bestowed** means granted. The idea is to give freely or graciously. **The name** is hard to identify. It could be "Lord" in view of verse 11: "…every tongue shall confess that Jesus Christ is Lord" (also see Acts 2:36). It is also possible that "the name" is not a proper name or title, but simply denotes authority or rank. **Every name** is all-inclusive. "Every name…every knee…every tongue" (vv. 9, 10, 11).

The implication is that the Philippians could also expect to be exalted by God if they would follow Christ's example and humble themselves.

10) So that at the name of Jesus every knee should bow, in heaven and on earth and under the earth.

At the name of Jesus would suggest a time when the name was uttered. However, the more literal translation is "in the name of Jesus" (Goodspeed), which suggests the sphere of all the name represents. **Every knee should bow** denotes devotion and submission. This imagery is taken from Isaiah 45:23, where it is applied to Yahweh. To bow in the name of Jesus is to declare His deity. **In heaven** refers to the angels. **On earth** refers to the living. **Under the earth** refers to the dead. This last group includes the fallen angels (2 Peter 2:4; Jude 6). The idea is one of universal acknowledgement. This will take place at the Second Coming.

11) And every tongue confess that Jesus Christ is Lord, to the glory of God the Father.

Every tongue confess indicates verbal acknowledgement. The bowing knee and confessing tongue are parallel, and encompass the totality of honor that Christ will receive at His coming. **Jesus Christ is Lord** is a central theme of the New Testament (Acts 2:36; Romans 10:9; 1 Corinthians 8:6; 12:3; Colossians 2:6). To confess that Jesus Christ is Lord is to declare His deity.

> Whenever the Jews read from Scripture, they considered the name of God, Yahweh, so sacred that they would substitute the term *adonai*. The Greek translation of *adonai* is *kurios*, which is rendered "Lord." Every tongue shall confess the divinity of Christ, which points to His sovereign reign over all creation. He possesses all glory, power, and authority. (16)

To the glory of God the Father shows that there is no rivalry between the Father and Son. Whenever the Son is honored, the Father is glorified.

It is interesting to note that the Jehovah's Witnesses translate the Greek word *kurios* as "Jehovah" in their New World Translation (NWT), except for in this text because *kurios* obviously refers to Jesus Christ. This is a clear example of the biasness of the NWT translators.

SHINING
(vv. 12-18)

12) Therefore, my beloved, as you have always obeyed, so now, not only as in my presence but much more in my absence, work out your own salvation with fear and trembling.

Christ's example of humility was described as an act of obedience in verse 8. Now Paul focused on the need for their obedience. **My beloved** is a term of endearment. The NIV says "my dear friends." This is another warm expression for those whom he longed for with the affection of Christ (1:8). **Obeyed** is parallel to "work out." **As you have always obeyed** refers to their past actions. They had a history of obedience. **Presence...absence** has already been contemplated in 1:27. **Work out** is present tense, and denotes continuous action. The NIV says "continue to work out." The idea is work out to the finish. **Your own** emphasizes individual responsibility. **Salvation** refers to eternal salvation. The same word was used of deliverance from prison in 1:19. Free-will is implied in this verse.

There is a saving work which God only can do for you; but there is also a work which you must do for yourselves. The work of your salvation is not completed in God's work in you. God's work must be carried out by yourselves. (17)

Fear and trembling denotes reverential awe. "Trembling" is the Greek word *tromou*, from which we get our English word "tremor." These terms appear together in three other Pauline letters (1 Corinthians 2:3; 2 Corinthians 7:15; Ephesians 6:5).

13) For it is God who works in you, both to will and to work for his good pleasure.

Paul shifted from their work to God's work. Paul already said that God began a good work in them and would bring it to completion (1:6). **Who works** is present tense, and denotes continuous action. The idea is that God is always at work. God works *in* and we work *out*. **Works** is the Greek word *energon*, from which we get our English word "energy." God's divine energy is at work within the Christian! **To will** refers to purpose or resolution. **To work** refers to the active response of believers to the in-working of God.

The paradoxical-truth of verses 12-13 is clear: while salvation depends wholly on God, one cannot be saved without doing his part. Jude made this point when he said that Christians were kept for Jesus Christ (v. 1) so long as they kept themselves in the love of God (v. 21).

14) Do all things without grumbling or questioning.

Grumbling denotes complaining. The same word is used in Acts 6:1, where the Hellenists made a complaint against the Hebrews. The ancient Israelites are a prime example of grumblers (1 Corinthians 10:10). **Questioning** denotes arguing. The same word is used in Luke 9:46, where the disciples argued about who was the greatest. It is from this Greek word *(dialogismon)* that we get our English word "dialogue." Grumbling and questioning will lead to division within a local church, which was apparently already happening at Philippi.

15) That you may be blameless and innocent, children of God without blemish in the midst of a crooked and twisted generation, among whom you shine as lights in the world.

In verses 15-16, Paul set forth three reasons why the Philippians should not grumble or question: for them, for unbelievers, and for Paul. **Blameless** means free from fault. It denotes living in a way as to not be rightly accused. **Innocent** means pure. The word was used of wine that had not been diluted with water. Hence, it denotes being morally unmixed. **Children of God** denotes their spiritual relationship to the Father. When the Philippians obeyed the gospel, they were adopted into the family of God and became His children. **Without blemish** means faultless. **Crooked and twisted** are complementary expressions, and refer to moral perverseness. Phillips says "warped and diseased." "Crooked" is from the Greek word *skolias*, from which we get our English word "scoliosis." Peter used this word in Acts 2:40, where he told the Jews to save themselves from their crooked generation. **Generation** refers to their contemporaries.

> Jesus denounced His contemporaries as "a wicked
> and adulterous generation" (Matt. 16:4), as a "faithless
> and perverse generation" (Matt. 17:17). The passage in
> Philippians is an echo of this. And how sadly true are
> these words as applied to our generation! (18)

Lights means luminaries. The NIV says "like stars in the
sky." **In the world** is the sphere of moral darkness. The Philippians were to let their influence shine in the moral darkness
around them. Jesus, the ultimate light in the world (John 1:4;
8:12), calls on His followers to be lights (Matthew 5:16; Ephesians 5:8; 1 Thessalonians 5:5). The language of this verse was
borrowed from the Song of Moses (Deuteronomy 32:5).

It is important to note that Paul did not tell the Philippians to
withdraw from the world and go into isolation. Christians are to
be in the world but not of the world (see John 17:15).

**16) Holding fast to the word of life, so that in the day
of Christ I may be proud that I did not run in vain or labor
in vain.**

In order to be lights in the world (v. 15), the Philippians had
to hold fast to the word of life. **Holding fast** means to hold firmly. **The word of life** is the body of truth. It is called the word of
life because it is the word that brings life. **The day of Christ**
is the Second Coming (1:6, 10). Paul had no doubt that the day
of Christ would come. **Proud** means to boast. This Greek word

(kauchema) is translated "glory" in 1:26. **Run** is an athletic metaphor (see 1 Corinthians 9:24, 26; Galatians 2:2; 5:7; 2 Timothy 4:7; Hebrews 12:1). In 3:12-14, Paul had the same imagery in mind when he spoke of "pressing forward." **Vain** means empty or for nothing.

> "Run in vain" portrays an athlete who, after enduring strict training and extreme exertion, finishes his race only to discover that he has been disqualified (1 Cor. 9:27). All of his hard work is for nothing! (19)

Although Paul's personal salvation was not dependent upon their continued faithfulness, he would feel that his efforts were wasted if they did not remain faithful. **Labor** means toil. The word denotes toiling in spite of great difficulty to the point of exhaustion.

17) Even if I am to be poured out as a drink offering upon the sacrificial offering of your faith, I am glad and rejoice with you all.

Like his Lord, Paul was willing to be "obedient to the point of death" (v. 8). **Even if** indicates uncertainty. Paul was confident that he would be released, but he was not absolutely certain of it (v. 23). **Poured out as a drink offering** also appears in 2 Timothy 4:6. In both places, Paul spoke metaphorically of his death. The drink offering of the Jews was the final act of the sacrificial ceremony. Paul knew that his life could be in its final stages depending on the verdict. **The sacrificial offering of your faith** refers to the monetary support prompted by their faith. This is another example of Paul's humility. He compared his sacrifice to the drink offering and their sacrifice to the main offering. **I am glad and rejoice** is a keynote of the letter. Dying for Christ did not bring him sadness, but happiness. **All** includes every member. Rather than grumbling (v. 14), the apostle was glad! "Glad and rejoice with you...Glad and rejoice with me" (vv. 17, 18).

18) Likewise you also should be glad and rejoice with me.

Paul wanted the Philippians to share in his joy. **Likewise** means in the same way. They were not to become discouraged at the prospect of the apostle's death or by their own circumstances, but were to imitate his optimism.

SENDING

(vv. 19-30)

At this point, Paul turned his attention to the travel plans of two co-workers: Timothy and Epaphroditus. Both of these brothers were very dear to Paul and to the Philippian church. Chronologically, the order is reversed. Paul began with Timothy even though Epaphroditus left first. It is interesting to note that Paul was a full-Jew, Timothy was a half-Jew, and Epaphroditus was no Jew at all. Yet they were all "the Israel of God" (Galatians 6:16).

19) I hope in the Lord Jesus to send Timothy to you soon, so that I too may be cheered by news of you.

Hope denotes confident expectation. **In the Lord** is the sphere of his hope. **To send Timothy** implies that Timothy was willing to be sent. He was with Paul at the founding of the Philippian church and when this letter was written (1:1). Paul hoped to send Timothy to them in the near future, but not until he knew the outcome of his trial (v. 23). Timothy's coming was not only for their sakes, but also for Paul's sake. He anticipated the return of Timothy with good news of the Philippian situation. **Cheered** literally means well-souled. The idea is in good spirits. This is reminiscent of 1 Thessalonians 3:6-7, where Timothy had visited the Thessalonian church and brought back good news that comforted the apostle.

Timothy was a young man from Lystra. His mother and grandmother had taught him the scriptures from childhood (2 Timothy 1:5; 3:15) and instilled in him a deep respect for God. Timothy was probably converted to Christ by Paul since the apostle referred to Timothy as a "child" (1 Corinthians 4:17; 1 Timothy 1:2; 2 Timothy 1:2). Timothy's actual father was a Greek. To avoid unnecessary tension in Jewish circles, Paul circumcised Timothy when he joined the missionary team (Acts 16:3). Paul had so much confidence in Timothy that he often sent him to address concerns within the churches (1 Corinthians 4:17; Philippians 2:19; 1 Thessalonians 3:2; 1 Timothy 1:3). He was Paul's troubleshooter! We know that Timothy was imprisoned at least once for the sake of the gospel (Hebrews 13:23) and, according to tradition, was martyred in Ephesus.

Timothy was the celebrated disciple of St. Paul, and bishop of Ephesus, where he zealously governed the Church until A.D. 97. At this period, as the pagans were about to celebrate a feast called Catagogion, Timothy, meeting the procession, severely reproved them for their ridiculous idolatry, which so exasperated the people that they fell upon him with their clubs, and beat him in so dreadful a manner that he expired of the bruises two days later. (20)

Timothy is mentioned with Paul in the opening greeting of six letters (2 Corinthians 1:1; Philippians 1:1; Colossians 1:1; 1 Thessalonians 1:1; 2 Thessalonians 1:1; Philemon 1), and was the recipient of two letters in the New Testament (1 Timothy and 2 Timothy).

20) For I have no one like him, who will be genuinely concerned for your welfare.

Although they already knew Timothy, Paul highly commended his co-worker to the Philippians. **Like him** is translated "of kindred spirit" in the NASB. **Genuinely** means legitimately or sincerely. **Concerned** is from the Greek word *merimnesei*, which can have both negative and positive connotations. It can mean to be anxious (negative) or to be concerned (positive). *Merimnesei* is used in a negative sense in 4:6. Timothy shared Paul's concern for the Philippians.

21) They all seek their own interests, not those of Jesus Christ.

Whereas Timothy had the interests of others in mind (v. 20), many had their own interests in mind. **They** probably refers to the preachers in Rome who opposed Paul. Such men were in violation of what Paul said in 2:4: "Let each of you look not only to his own interests, but also to the interests of others." One cannot seek the interests of Christ while at the same time seeking his own interests. This may have been intended as an indirect rebuke to the Philippians.

> In a very real sense, all of us live either in Philippians 1:21 or Philippians 2:21! (21)

22) But you know Timothy's proven worth, how as a son with a father he has served with me in the gospel.

You know indicates personal knowledge. Timothy had been loyal to Paul as a son is to his father. **Proven worth** refers to character that has been tested or tried. Another form of this word is translated "approve" in 1:10. **As a son with a father** is a strong illustration that stresses faithfulness. Timothy worked together with Paul for the cause of the gospel.

23) I hope therefore to send him just as soon as I see how it will go with me.

Hope denotes confident expectation (see v. 19). Paul had not received direct revelation about the outcome of his trial. He planned to send Timothy to Philippi, but not until he knew what would happen with his situation. Goodspeed says "just as soon as I see how my case is going to turn out."

24) And I trust in the Lord that shortly I myself will come also.

In addition to Timothy's coming, Paul also hoped to come soon. **Trust** denotes confidence (see 1:6). **In the Lord** is the sphere of his trust. We know that Paul did ultimately return to Philippi.

Epaphroditus was sent by the Philippian church to Paul with financial support and to lend his assistance to the prisoner. Paul referred to Epaphroditus in impressive fashion: brother, fellow worker, fellow soldier, messenger, and minister. These five descriptions can be divided into two parts: Epaphroditus' relation to Paul (first three) and Epaphroditus' relation to the Philippians (last two). Paul also said that Epaphroditus risked his life to do the work (v. 30).

25) I have thought it necessary to send to you Epaphroditus my brother and fellow worker and fellow soldier, and your messenger and minister to my need.

Although the brother from Philippi was a great asset to Paul during his imprisonment, the apostle decided to send him back home for the good of others. This is an example of Paul's selflessness. **Necessary** means needful. **Epaphroditus**, which means lovely, was a common name. However, it only appears two times in the New Testament, both in this letter (2:25; 4:18). Epaphroditus was a Christian from Philippi who brought monetary support to Paul with the understanding that he would stay as an assistant. Based on an inscription which reads "Gauis Claudius

Epaphroditus," some have suggested that Epaphroditus may be the Macedonian "Gaius" in Acts 19:29. Although Epaphras is a contraction of Epaphroditus, we should not confuse the Philippian brother with the Colossian brother (Colossians 1:7; 4:12; Philemon 23). We do not know anything else about Epaphroditus' background. **My** indicates that the first three descriptions were in relation to Paul. **Brother** denotes spiritual kinship (see 1:12). They were both children of God. **Fellow worker** denotes common labor. They worked side by side. This Greek word *(synergon)* appears again in 4:3 (also see Romans 16:3, 9, 21; 1 Thessalonians 3:2; Philemon 1, 24). **Fellow soldier** denotes common warfare. They fought side by side. Christians are spiritual soldiers (Philippians 2:25; 2 Timothy 2:3-4; Philemon 2) and are to be arrayed in spiritual armor (Ephesians 6:10-18; 1 Thessalonians 5:8). They are to fight the good fight (1 Timothy 6:12; 2 Timothy 4:7).

> There is, perhaps, a progression of terms here: Some are brothers, but not workers. Some are brothers and workers, but they will not fight for the truth, always endeavoring to avoid controversy. The ideal Christian, though, possesses all of the above traits; he is balanced! (22)

Based on the above descriptions, it is obvious that Epaphroditus was more valuable to Paul than the money he brought. **Your** indicates that the last two descriptions were in relation to the Philippians. **Messenger** is the Greek word *apostolon*, and is often translated "apostle" in the New Testament. The word means "one sent," and is used in both a general and technical sense. It is used in a general sense in Acts 14:14, 2 Corinthians 8:23, and

Galatians 1:19. Paul referred to Epaphroditus as "your" apostle, not "Christ's" apostle. **Minister** means servant. Perhaps Paul felt the need to commend Epaphroditus because he feared that the Philippians would criticize him for returning early.

26) For he has been longing for you all and has been distressed because you heard that he was ill.

Paul explained why he was sending Epaphroditus home. **Longing for** denotes strong desire; to yearn for (see 1:8; 4:1). Phillips says "he has been home-sick for you." **All** includes every member. **Distressed** means to be agonized or troubled. The same word *(ademonon)* is used of the Lord's agony in the garden of Gethsemane (Matthew 26:37). Epaphroditus had become very sick to the point of death (vv. 27, 30) and the Philippians knew about it. Therefore, in addition to being home-sick he was also concerned that they were concerned. **You heard that he was ill** implies that a messenger had arrived in Rome and informed Epaphroditus of the Philippian's concern. We are not told what made Epaphroditus sick or how the church back home found out about it. Apparently there was no need to explain such details. Paul's decision to send his trusted helper back home is a great example of putting the interests of others first (v. 4).

27) Indeed he was ill, near to death. But God had mercy on him, and not only on him but on me also, lest I should have sorrow upon sorrow.

Paul verified that the report was not exaggerated. Epaphroditus' condition was very serious. **Near to death** parallels "nearly died" in verse 30. **God had mercy on him** credits God with Epaphroditus' recovery. **Mercy** means compassion or pity. Apparently Paul did not miraculously heal his brother, but God providentially brought about healing. The apostles did not miraculously heal all who were sick in the New Testament (1 Timothy 5:23; 2 Timothy 4:20). In fact, Paul himself had an affliction that was not removed (2 Corinthians 12:7-10). **On me also** indicates that Paul viewed Epaphroditus' recovery as mercy bestowed on him. **Sorrow upon sorrow** denotes escalation of sorrow. God's Word Translation says "having one sorrow on top of another." Paul was in chains, uncertain of his future, knew that some preachers were trying to harm him, and feeling the infirmities of old age (Philemon 9); not to mention the "daily pressure" of his concern for all the churches (2 Corinthians 11:28). If his beloved brother had died, the pain would have been an overwhelming burden.

28) I am the more eager to send him, therefore, that you may rejoice at seeing him again, and that I may be less anxious.

As noted, Paul put aside his own interests and felt it best to send Epaphroditus home. **The more eager** denotes special urgency. **That you may rejoice** was the projected benefit for the Philippians. **That I may be less anxious** was the projected benefit for Paul. **Less anxious** means less grieved or sorrowful. Paul's anxiety would be lessened but not eliminated.

29) So receive him in the Lord with all joy, and honor such men.

Receive him in the Lord means to accept him favorably. This is intended to ensure that Epaphroditus received a heroes welcome in Philippi, and is reminiscent of Romans 16:2, where Paul told the brethren to receive Phoebe in the Lord and adds "in a way worthy of the saints." **With all joy** as opposed to with all disappointment. **Honor such men** means to regard men of his caliber as precious or prized. Most believe that Paul was trying to prevent criticism from the brethren.

30) For he nearly died for the work of Christ, risking his life to complete what was lacking in your service to me.

Paul gave them a good reason to honor Epaphroditus--He almost died for the cause of Christ. **Nearly died** parallels "near to death" in verse 27. **Risking his life** denotes the perilous nature of the work he performed. Epaphroditus exposed himself to real harm. Either on his way to Rome or once he arrived there, Epaphroditus had become very sick. He was in grave condition. "Risking his life" is reminiscent of Acts 15:26, where Paul and Barnabas were said to have risked their lives for the sake of Jesus Christ, and Romans 16:4, where Prisca and Aquila were said to have risked their necks for Paul. **To complete what was lacking in your service** sums up the reason why Epaphroditus risked his life for the apostle. This is not a criticism of the Philippians. They were not derelict but deficient. The NRSV says "to make up for those services that you could not give me."

CHAPTER THREE

SECURING

(vv. 1-3)

The Philippian church was not immune from an element that plagued many of the early churches--Judaizers. Judaizers were Jewish Christians who tried to bind parts of the Old Law, especially circumcision, upon Gentiles (Acts 15:1, 5). They were guilty of trusting in the flesh, binding a law that was obsolete, and denying the all-sufficiency of the gospel for salvation. Paul dealt very strongly with Judaizers (Galatians 5:12). His warning was designed to secure the brethren from this dangerous element.

We are not told how Paul was made aware of the threat posed by the Judaizers. He may have received divine revelation or the news may have come through a human messenger (see 2:26). Regardless, he took the threat very seriously. His tone was very poignant. He did not mince words!

This chapter can be divided into three parts: Paul's past (vv. 1-11), Paul's present (vv. 12-19), and Paul's future (vv. 20-21).

1) Finally, my brothers, rejoice in the Lord. To write the same things to you is no trouble to me and is safe for you.

Finally is from the Greek word *loipon,* which can be a transition word. Therefore, Paul probably did not mean to say "in conclusion" but rather "furthermore" or "as to the rest."

It is wholly needless to understand Paul as about to finish and then suddenly changing his mind like some preachers who announce the end a half dozen times. (23)

My brothers is a familiar term of affection (see 1:12). **Rejoice** is a keynote of the letter. **In the Lord** is the sphere of their joy. This phrase appears again in 4:4. **To write the same things** could refer to what preceded (rejoice in the Lord) or to what follows (beware of false teachers). It probably refers to what he was about to say about false teachers. He went on to write, "For many, of whom I have often told you and now tell you even with tears" (v. 18). Like Peter (2 Peter 1:13; 3:1), Paul knew the value of repetition. **Trouble** means irksome or tedious. **Safe for you** means for their safety. This is yet another example of Paul looking out for the interests of others (2:4).

2) Look out for the dogs, look out for the evildoers, look out for those who mutilate the flesh.

Paul addressed a potential threat to the Philippian congregation--Judaizers. All three descriptions refer to the same group. The language is strong and penetrating. **Look out** means take heed or be on guard. This Greek word *(blepete)* appears in Mark 8:15 and 12:38, where it is translated "beware." Each of these three derogatory descriptions begin with this warning to indicate urgency. Paul called them dogs (character), evildoers (conduct), and mutilation (creed). **Dogs** were scavengers who roamed in packs and ate garbage, and therefore, became a term of reproach (Matthew 7:6). Jews often referred to Gentiles as dogs.

The Jews referred to the Gentiles as dogs for at least three reasons. First, this association was made because of the Gentiles' food choices. The Jews were restricted to a kosher diet according to the Law, while the Gentiles (like dogs) ate anything they desired...Second, the Gentiles were also compared to dogs because of their gross immorality. They sometimes behaved like dogs, following their own passions and desires without restraint...Third, the Jews also viewed the Gentiles as being on a lower level because they were not part of the covenant. God gave the Law to His chosen people Israel, not to the Gentile dogs. (24)

Paul used their insult against them. Obviously, his warning was against two-legged dogs! **Evildoers** is the second stinging insult to the Judaizers. Although they considered their insistence on the Old Law to be good, it was really evil. Their insistence on the Old Law was a denial of the all-sufficiency of the gospel for salvation. In 2 Corinthians 11:13, Paul called this same group "deceitful workmen." **Those who mutilate the flesh** is the third stinging insult to the Judaizers. Circumcision was the sign of the covenant made with Abraham and was a vital part of the Jewish religion. However, it was wrong to bind circumcision on Christians (Galatians 5:1-13). In Christ, it does not matter whether or not one is physically circumcised (1 Corinthians 7:19; Galatians 6:15). The Judaizers were binding circumcision as a means of justification before God, which Paul could not allow. Rather than calling them "the circumcision," the apostle sarcastically called them "the mutilation" (NKJV).

One cannot help but be impressed with the militant tone of verse 2. Paul was harsh in his treatment of false teachers, as were many other biblical figures. For instance, Elijah mocked the prophets of Baal suggesting that their god was "using the toilet" (1 Kings 18:27, CEV) and had them slaughtered (v. 40); John the baptizer called the Pharisees and Sadducees "a brood of vipers" (Matthew 3:7); Peter went on a "righteous tirade" describing false teachers in 2 Peter 2; and, according to tradition, John hurriedly left a public bath in Ephesus when the heretic Cerinthus entered, exclaiming, "Let us fly, lest even the bath house fall down, for Cerinthus, the enemy of truth is within!" Perhaps the best example is the Lord Jesus in Matthew 23. He described the scribes and Pharisees as "hypocrites," "blind fools," "brood of vipers," etc. Therefore, it should not surprise us that Paul wished the Judaizers would "emasculate themselves" (Galatians 5:12) and called them "enemies of the cross" (Philippians 3:18).

3) For we are the circumcision, who worship by the Spirit of God and glory in Christ Jesus and put no confidence in the flesh.

Jews were commonly identified as "the circumcised" while Gentiles were called "the uncircumcised" (Galatians 2:7-9). Having referred to the Judaizers as dogs, evildoers, and those who mutilate the flesh, Paul claimed that Christians are the true circumcision. **We** refers to Paul and the saints in Philippi. **The circumcision** was the proud title of the Jews that Paul applied to Christians (see Romans 2:28-29; Galatians 6:16). Christians are the true circumcision because of three distinct qualities: they worship by the Spirit of God, glory in Christ Jesus, and put no confidence in the flesh. **Worship by the Spirit of God** means they relied on the Holy Spirit's guidance in service rendered to God. They followed His instructions made known by the apostles and other inspired teachers. **Glory in Christ Jesus** means they made Christ the source of their boasting. **Put no confidence in the flesh** means they did not put trust in their own achievements. These three things are put in contrast to the Judaizers who relied on their flesh, gloried in their flesh, and put confidence in their flesh.

As noted, Judaizers were Jewish Christians who tried to bind parts of the Old Law on Christians. There are many people today who follow in their footsteps, binding such things as tithing, the Sabbath, certain dietary restrictions, etc. Hence, they are "neo-Judaizers!"

SURPASSING

(vv. 4-11)

Since Paul was confronting Jewish Christians who gloried in their Jewish heritage and achievements, it was necessary for the apostle to show that he surpassed them all in such areas. He was second to none! If anyone had reason to put confidence in the flesh, it was Paul (see Galatians 1:14).

There are seven items mentioned in this particular list of credentials. The first four were by virtue of birth while the last three were personal achievements. This section is similar to 2

Corinthians 11:16-33, where Paul felt compelled to show that his achievements surpassed those of his opponents.

4) Though I myself have reason for confidence in the flesh also. If anyone else thinks he has reason for confidence in the flesh, I have more.

Paul had more reason to put confidence in the flesh than his opponents. His credentials trumped their credentials. **Anyone else** refers primarily to the Judaizers. **I have more** emphasizes his superiority in this area. Paul did not mean that he trusted in the flesh, but was merely suggesting that if anyone had the right to do so, it was him.

5) Circumcised on the eighth day, of the people of Israel, of the tribe of Benjamin, a Hebrew of Hebrews; as to the law, a Pharisee.

Paul gave examples to demonstrate that if anyone had the right to put confidence in the flesh, it was him. As noted, the first four were by virtue of birth while the last three were personal achievements. **Circumcised on the eighth day** is literally "an eighth day man." Paul had been circumcised on the eighth day, not at age 13 like the Ishmaelites or as an adult like Gentile proselytes. John the baptizer (Luke 1:59) and Jesus (Luke 2:21) were circumcised on the eighth day. **Of the people of Israel** means that he was of that race or stock. He was not a proselyte. **Of the tribe of Benjamin** builds upon the previous credential. Not only was he of the people of Israel, but of a prominent tribe. Benjamin was a son of Rachel, Israel's first king was a Benjaminite, etc. Paul mentioned his Benjaminite background in Acts 13:21 and Romans 11:1. **A Hebrew of Hebrews** probably means that both of his parents were Hebrews ("Hebrews" is plural) who retained the language and custom. He was not of mixed parentage (see Acts 16:1). **A Pharisee** means that he was part of the strictest sect among the Jews (Acts 26:5). The Pharisees were one of many sects that developed during the inter-testament period, the 400 years of silence between Malachi and Matthew, along with the Sadducees, Herodians, Essenes, etc. The word "Pharisee," which means separate ones, appears only here outside of the Gospels and Acts. There were about 6,000 Pharisees at the time of Jesus' birth. In Acts 23:6, Paul said, "I am a Pharisee, a son of Pharisees."

6) As to zeal, a persecutor of the church; as to righteousness under the law, blameless.

Zeal denotes fervor. **Persecutor of the church** means that he harassed or troubled the church. The word denotes one who presses or pursues. (The same word is translated "press" in 3:12). Paul was a spiritual terrorist before his conversion (Acts 7:58; 8:1, 3; 9:1-9; 22:4; 26:9-11; Galatians 1:13, 23; 1 Timothy 1:15). **Church** is from a Greek word *(ekklesia)* that means assembly. The word was not inherently religious, and was used of any assembly (Acts 19:32, 39, 41). The New Testament speaks of the Lord's church in two senses--universal and local. The universal church consists of all the saved (Matthew 16:18) while the local church consists of the saved who work and worship together in a particular location (1 Corinthians 1:2). Local churches were organized with elders and deacons (see 1:1). Paul was speaking of the Lord's church in its universal sense in this text. The only other time this word appears in this letter is in 4:15, where it is used in a local sense. Though it hurt Paul to think about his former life as a persecutor (1 Corinthians 15:9; 1 Timothy 1:15), it demonstrated clearly his Jewish zeal. At the time, he probably felt like Phinehas in Numbers 25, who was commended for aggressively pursuing apostates in the camp. **Righteousness** means to be declared as right. **Blameless** means without fault. This does not mean that Paul was sinless (see 3:12), but that he was obedient to the Law of Moses.

7) But whatever gain I had, I counted as loss for the sake of Christ.

Paul now explained that his Jewish credentials were of no advantage in Christ. **Whatever gain I had** refers to his achievements in Judaism. **I counted as loss** means they were regarded as of no value. **For the sake of Christ** means on account of his surrender to Christ.

8) Indeed, I count everything as loss because of the surpassing worth of knowing Christ Jesus my Lord. For his sake I have suffered the loss of all things and count them as rubbish, in order that I may gain Christ.

Paul increased the scope of things counted as loss for Christ. **Everything** includes any person, place, or thing in which one may put his confidence. **Knowing Christ Jesus** does not merely refer to knowledge about Christ. It denotes knowledge gained by experience. **My Lord** is reminiscent of 1:3 and 4:19, where

Paul said "my God." It emphasizes personal relationship. **The loss of all things** that he might previously have counted as gain. This would encourage the Philippians who were suffering loss as well (1:28-30). **Rubbish** means garbage.

9) And be found in him, not having a righteousness of my own that comes from the law, but that which comes through faith in Christ, the righteousness from God that depends on faith.

Found in him refers to his spiritual condition. Paul hoped to be found in possession of his profession--Jesus Christ! **Righteousness** means to be declared as right. Paul did not attempt to obtain righteousness through the Old Law, which was impossible (Galatians 2:16), but through faith in Christ. **That depends on faith** denotes more than mental assent. The idea is obedient submission to Him. Paul began and ended the Roman letter with a reference to "the obedience of faith" (Romans 1:5; 16:26).

10) That I may know him and the power of his resurrection, and may share his sufferings, becoming like him in his death.

Paul knew Christ very well. However, he looked forward to certain experiences that would enhance that knowledge. **That I may know him** refers not to intellectual knowledge but to experimental knowledge (see v. 8). **Power** is from the Greek word *dynamin*, from which we get our English word "dynamite." This refers to the power of God that raised Christ from the dead, which is appropriated to Christians by faith (Ephesians 1:18-20).

Share is from the Greek word *koinonian*, which appears several times in this letter. This refers to association with or participation in His sufferings. **Becoming like him in his death** may be a reference to the possible verdict of Paul's case. Paul would die a similar death to that of his Savior.

11) That by any means possible I may attain the resurrection from the dead.

Attain means to acquire. **The resurrection from the dead** refers to the resurrection of the righteous when the Lord returns (1 Thessalonians 4:16). Though all the dead will be raised in judgment at that time (John 5:28-29; Acts 24:15), Paul anticipated the benefits of being among the saved, that is, those raised to eternal life in heaven. Throughout this letter Paul has referenced the Second Coming of Christ (1:6, 10; 2:16).

STRAINING
(vv. 12-21)

12) Not that I have already obtained this or am already perfect, but I press on to make it my own, because Christ Jesus has made me his own.

Rather than resting on past achievements that are of no value, Paul pressed forward. **Not that** appears two other times in the letter, both in chapter four (4:11, 17). **Already obtained this** refers to the goals expressed before. **Perfect** denotes a permanent state of perfection.

> Paul pointedly denies that he has reached a spiritual impasse of non-development. Certainly he knew nothing of so-called sudden absolute perfection by any single experience. Paul has made great progress in Christlikeness, but the goal is still before him, not behind him. (25)

I press on appears again in verse 14, and means to pursue or strive for. The same Greek word was translated "persecutor" in verse 6. Paul was a man of metaphors (builder, farmer, athlete, etc). Here he used an athletic metaphor of running a race. A few years later as he neared execution, Paul wrote, "I have finished the race" (2 Timothy 4:7). **Christ Jesus has made me his own** is a reference to the time of his conversion when Jesus appeared to him on the road to Damascus and sent him into the city where he was baptized (Acts 9:1-19; 22:1-16; 26:12-18). "Make it my own… made me his own" is an obvious play on words.

13) Brothers, I do not consider that I have made it my own. But one thing I do: forgetting what lies behind and straining forward to what lies ahead.

Brothers is an affectionate term that denotes their spiritual kinship. **Forgetting what lies behind** refers to past achievements in Christ. By this time, Paul had done extensive traveling, preaching, planting, suffering, writing, etc. for the gospel. However, he did not dwell on the past but focused on the future. No successful runner spends his time looking back! **Straining for-ward** pictures a runner stretching forth for the finish line. **What lies ahead** refers to the finish line, that is, eternal life (Hebrews 12:1-2). Verses 12-13 follow a "not...but" pattern.

14) I press on toward the goal for the prize of the up-ward call of God in Christ Jesus.

I press on appeared in verse 12. **The goal** refers to the post which was placed at the finish line. **The prize** is eternal life (see 1 Corinthians 9:24). **Of God** means He is the source. **In Christ Jesus** is the sphere.

> Missing in Paul's metaphor of racing are other runners since each Christian has his own race to run. Believers are to spur one another on rather than com-peting with each other. One does not win the prize by crossing the finish line first. Instead, an individual will be rewarded for faithfully finishing the race. (26)

15) Let those of us who are mature think this way, and if in anything you think otherwise, God will reveal that also to you.

Although Paul was not perfect (v. 12), he was mature in the faith. **Mature** refers to spiritual adulthood. Paul urged those who have reached adulthood in their spirituality to think this way. **This way** refers to the need to continue pressing ahead re-gardless of past achievements. If any of the brothers were immature in their thinking, God would reveal it to them. Just how God would reveal it to them is not stated. James 1:5 indicates that those who lacked wisdom were to pray for it. **Reveal** means to disclose or uncover.

16) Only let us hold true to what we have attained.

Hold true means to keep in step with. **What we have attained** is the maturity level each possessed at that time. The JNT says "Only let our conduct fit the level we have already attained."

17) Brothers, join in imitating me, and keep your eyes on those who walk according to the example you have in us.

Brothers is an affectionate term that denotes their spiritual kinship. **Join in imitating me** means they were to follow Paul's example. The compound word used here is *symmimetai*, which is the preposition "with" *(sym)* and the noun "imitator" *(mimetic)*. It is from this Greek word that we get our English word "mimic." Paul often urged brethren to imitate his example even as he imitated Christ's example (1 Corinthians 11:1; also see 1 Corinthians 4:16; 2 Thessalonians 3:7-9). **Keep your eyes on** is from the Greek word *skopeite*, from which we get our English word "scope." The idea is to observe closely or stay fixed on. The same word is used in Romans 16:17, where Paul told the Romans to watch out for divisive brothers. **Walk** means live. These "walkers" stand in sharp contrast to those of the next verse. **Example** is from the Greek word *typon*, which is translated "pattern" in

Hebrews 8:5. The Philippians were to keep their eyes focused on those who lived according to the same example (or pattern) of Paul.

18) For many, of whom I have often told you and now tell you even with tears, walk as enemies of the cross of Christ.

Many probably refers to the Judaizers (v. 2). **Of whom I have often told you** means they had been warned of such people in the past. **Now tell you** in this present letter. **Even with tears** shows the degree of concern with which the warning was made. It was not uncommon for Paul to shed tears in the New Testament (Acts 20:19, 31; Romans 9:2; 2 Corinthians 2:4). **Enemy** refers to one who is hostile. The same word is used in Acts 13:10, where Elymas is called "enemy of unrighteousness." Though the Judaizers claimed to follow Christ, they were His enemies. **The cross of Christ** is used by metonymy in which the part stands for the whole. The cross represents the entire faith of the gospel. Anyone who would oppose or pervert the gospel is an enemy of the cross of Christ. Interestingly, Polycarp used similar language when he wrote to the Philippians: "the enemies of the cross."

19) Their end is destruction, their god is their belly, and they glory in their shame, with minds set on earthly things.

Paul used very strong language to describe the enemies of the cross. **End** refers to their final outcome. **Destruction** does not denote extinction but ruin. **Their god is their belly** may refer to the Judaizer's reliance on certain dietary restrictions of the Old Law. **They glory in their shame** may refer to the Judaizer's pride in circumcision. Such glorying is shameful because it makes Christ "of no advantage" (Galatians 5:2). The Judaizers gloried in the very things that Paul counted as "loss" (v. 8). **With minds set on earthly things** means they were consumed with the physical (diet, circumcision, etc). The contrast between the outcome of Christ's enemies in this verse and Christ's faithful in the next two verses could not be clearer.

Some suggest that Paul was referring to the sensuous influence of their pagan neighbors in the above verse. However, since moral laxness does not seem to have been a problem in the church of Philippi and the larger context, it seems best to view the aforementioned enemies as Judaizers.

20) But our citizenship is in heaven, and from it we await a Savior, the Lord Jesus Christ.

In contrast to the earthly-minded Judaizers whose end is destruction (v. 19), faithful Christians are citizens of heaven whose end is salvation. **Citizenship** or homeland (see NCV). **Heaven** is God's dwelling place. Christians are merely sojourners on the earth (1 Peter 2:11), awaiting the time we make it home to heaven. Our names are "enrolled in heaven" (Hebrews 12:23), and from it we derive our laws, rights, privileges, etc. **Await** denotes eager anticipation. Christians should look with haste for the coming of Christ (1 Corinthians 1:7; 1 Thessalonians 1:10; Titus 2:13; Hebrews 9:28; 2 Peter 3:12). **Savior** means deliverer. **Lord** denotes one in authority. To the Philippians, the words "citizenship," "savior," and "lord" would have Roman overtones. Roman citizenship was a prized possession and Caesar wore the titles savior and lord.

The earth is not eternal (2 Peter 3:7-12; also Genesis 8:22; Matthew 5:18; 24:35). Therefore, the focus of a Christian is not on earth, but in heaven: Our treasure is in heaven (Matthew 19:21), our citizenship is in heaven (Philippians 3:20), our hope is in heaven (Colossians 1:5), our inheritance is in heaven (1 Peter 1:4), etc.

21) Who will transform our lowly body to be like his glorious body, by the power that enables him even to subject all things to himself.

This verse clearly assumes a bodily resurrection that will coincide with a glorious transformation. **Transform** means to change. **Our** places Paul with the Philippians. **Lowly** means humble. Our fleshly bodies are incompatible for heavenly existence (1 Corinthians 15:50). **Like his glorious body** refers to the glorified body of Christ. It is immortal and fit for heaven. The same idea is expressed in 1 John 3:2, which says that when Christ appears "we shall be like him." **Power** is from the Greek word *energeian*, from which we get our English word "energy" (see 2:13). **All things** refers to all creation. The same power that enables Christ to subject all things to himself will also transform our lowly bodies to be like His glorious body.

CHAPTER FOUR

SQUABBLING

(vv. 1-3)

1) Therefore, my brothers, whom I love and long for, my joy and crown, stand firm thus in the Lord, my beloved.

My brothers is an affectionate term that denotes their spiritual kinship. **Love** is from the Greek word *agapetoi*, which is the highest form of love (see 1:9). **Long for** is reminiscent of 1:8, where Paul said he yearned for them. This denotes his strong desire to see the Philippians. In 2:26, Paul said that Epaphroditus had been "longing for" the brethren. **My joy** indicates that the Philippians were a source of joy for the apostle. **Crown** is from the Greek word *stephanos*, and refers to a victor's wreath. It was a wreath given to champions of athletic competitions. There is a different Greek word for the crown of royalty *(diadema)*. The New Testament writers often referred to the victor's crown in their writings (1 Corinthians 9:25; 1 Thessalonians 2:19; 2 Timothy 4:8; James 1:12; 1 Peter 5:4; Revelation 2:10; 3:11). In this verse, Christians were the crown. Paul used similar language to describe the Thessalonians at the Second Coming in 1 Thessalonians 2:19-20. **Stand firm** denotes steadfast persistence (also 1:27). Paul often called on congregations to stand firm (1 Corinthians 16:13; Galatians 5:1; Ephesians 6:13; 2 Thessalonians 2:15). **In the Lord** is the sphere of their standing. **My beloved** is another affectionate term. The NIV says "dear friends."

Before concluding the letter, Paul felt it necessary to address a problem within the congregation at Philippi. Two sisters were squabbling. The apostle urged the women to reconcile and asked others to help them. Unlike 1 Corinthians 1:11 where Paul identified his source ("For it has been reported to me by Chloe's people..."), it is unclear who told Paul about the problem. Perhaps Epaphroditus or some other visitor to Rome told him of the situation, or he may have received his information by inspiration.

Paul had emphasized the need for unity throughout the letter. Now, he makes direct reference to a certain situation. Although the conduct of Euodia and Syntyche was unbecoming of Christians, at least Paul considered them to be mature enough in the faith to call their names in a letter that would be read before the entire assembly (see Colossians 4:16; 1 Thessalonians 5:27; 1 Timothy 4:13).

2) I entreat Euodia and I entreat Syntyche to agree in the Lord.

Entreat means to encourage or exhort. Paul was careful to address each woman the same to avoid showing favoritism. **Euodia**, which means fragrant, was one squabbling sister. **Syntyche**, which means fortunate, was the other squabbling sister. The issue was not doctrinal in nature. If it were, Paul would have sided with whoever had the truth. However, in this dispute he remained neutral. It must have been a personality conflict of some sort. **Agree** means to be of the same mind. In 2:2, Paul said to be "of the same mind." These women are not mentioned elsewhere in scripture.

3) Yes, I ask you also, true companion, help these women, who have labored side by side with me in the gospel together with Clement and the rest of my fellow workers, whose names are in the book of life.

Paul called on another member to help the squabbling sisters. **True** means genuine. **Companion** is from the Greek word *Syzyge,* and means yokefellow. It is possible that the word should be left untranslated and viewed as a proper name. Several translations take that approach (NJB, JNT) while others add the option in a footnote. The fact that proper names appear immediately before (Euodia, Syntyche) and after (Clement) leads me to believe that this view is correct. **Help** means to aid or assist. **These women** are Euodia and Syntyche. **Who have labored** means they had worked hard with Paul in the gospel.

> Unfortunately, these Christian women had redirected their energies from fighting together for the cause of Christ to fighting one another. It was essential for the two ladies to mend their relationship and return to the work in which they were once engaged. (27)

Some have misused this passage to authorize women preachers. Although there is no such thing as a second-class citizen in the kingdom (Galatians 3:28), God has given men and women different roles. Women are not to "exercise authority over a man; rather, she is to remain quiet" (1 Timothy 2:12). Since preachers are to speak "with all authority" (Titus 2:15) and women are not to exercise authority over a man, it should go without saying that women preachers are not authorized in scripture. Euodia and Syntyche could have labored with Paul in many ways while still respecting their role.

Clement, which means merciful, was a co-worker with the others. Clement was a common name. It is not likely that he was Clement of Rome. **Fellow workers** refer to other Christians. This same word was used to describe Epaphroditus in 2:25. **The book of life** refers metaphorically to the heavenly record of the faithful; the list of those who belong to God. Many ancient civilizations kept a record of its citizens.

STABILIZING

(vv. 4-9)

4) Rejoice in the Lord always; again I will say, Rejoice.

This verse is reminiscent of 1:18, where Paul said, "Rejoice. Yes, and I will rejoice." **Rejoice** is present tense and denotes continual rejoicing. Though they were being persecuted and their beloved apostle was in chains, they should maintain their spirit of joy. **In the Lord** is the sphere of their joy. A Christian's joy is not dependent on outward circumstances but exists in spite of them (Acts 5:41; 16:25; 1 Peter 4:16).

5) Let your reasonableness be known to everyone. The Lord is at hand.

Reasonableness refers to a humble disposition that defers to others. The NIV says "gentleness." **Be known to everyone** by their conduct. **The Lord is at hand** can mean that He is nearby (proximity) or that He is coming soon (time). Both could be true. Jesus is ever-present and ever-ready to return. Paul spoke often of the Second Coming in this letter (1:6, 10; 2:10, 16; 3:20). It is possible, but less likely, that Paul was referring to the Lord coming in judgment against Jerusalem, which took place in A.D. 70.

6) Do not be anxious about anything, but in everything by prayer and supplication with thanksgiving let your requests be made known to God.

We have another "not this...but that" statement (see 2:3). **Anxious** means worried. Christians are told not to worry (Matthew 6:25, 31, 34; 1 Peter 5:7). The word was used in a good sense in 2:20, where it is translated "concerned." The Philippians had plenty of reasons to worry. They were poor, persecuted, threatened by false teachers, worried about Paul and Epaphroditus, dealing with squabbling sisters, etc. **Prayer and supplication** is the remedy to worry. Rather than worrying about anything, pray about everything! **With thanksgiving** means that we must approach God in prayer with an attitude of gratitude. This is similar to Colossians 4:2, where Paul said to be watchful in prayer "with thanksgiving." **Let your requests be made known** does not mean that God is unaware of what we need, He is aware (Matthew 6:8). It means that He wants us to ask Him, which proves our faith and dependence.

7) And the peace of God, which surpasses all under-standing, will guard your hearts and your minds in Christ Jesus.

The peace of God refers to the peace that God provides; He is its source. In Colossians 3:15, Paul mentioned "the peace of Christ." Peace is tranquility even in the midst of turmoil. The Philippians could have the peace of God while being persecuted. In verse 9, God is called "the God of peace." **Surpasses** means transcends or rises above. **Understanding** or comprehension. The peace of God is greater than man can even comprehend. **Guard** means to keep or protect. **Your hearts and your minds** refers to the places of emotion and intellect. **In Christ** is the sphere of the protection.

8) Finally, brothers, whatever is true, whatever is honor-able, whatever is just, whatever is pure, whatever is lovely, whatever is commendable, if there is any excellence, if there is anything worthy of praise, think about these things.

With a distinct rhetorical tone, Paul urged the Philippians to focus their minds on what is good. There are several "virtue" lists in the New Testament (Galatians 5:22-23; Colossians 3:12-17; 2 Peter 1:5-7). **True** means genuine or sincere. **Honorable** means dignified or noble. **Just** means fair or right. **Pure** means mor-ally blameless or unspotted. **Lovely** means beautiful or pleasing. **Commendable** means admirable or of good report. **Excellence** is from the Greek word *arete,* and refers to moral excellence. **Worthy of praise** in man's perception. Paul was saying to think on things that righteous men view as worthy of praise. **Think**

about these things means to dwell on or fill your thoughts with. "Think about these things...practice these things" (vv. 8-9).

9) What you have learned and received and heard and seen in me--practice these things, and the God of peace will be with you.

Learned and received and heard and seen in me are the different ways in which Paul taught them the truth. Put what you have attained into action! **Practice** is present tense and denotes continual practicing. The NRSV says "keep on doing." **The God of peace** is a common description of God (Romans 15:33; 16:20; 1 Corinthians 14:33; 2 Corinthians 13:11; 1 Thessalonians 5:23; 2 Thessalonians 3:16; Hebrews 13:20). It means that He is the God who brings peace; He is its source (see v. 7).

SUPPORTING
(vv. 10-23)

Preachers have the right to be supported by churches (1 Corinthians 9:1-14; 2 Thessalonians 3:9). The Philippian church sent financial support to Paul as he labored in the gospel, even during his confinement at Rome. Therefore, Paul expressed his appreciation for their fellowship.

10) I rejoiced in the Lord greatly that now at length you have revived your concern for me. You were indeed concerned for me, but you had no opportunity.

I rejoiced refers back to when Epaphroditus arrived with support. **In the Lord** is the sphere of his rejoicing. **Greatly** emphasizes the degree of his rejoicing. **Now at length** means at last. This indicates that a considerable amount of time had elapsed since the last time they sent support. **Revived** literally means to blossom again (see NEB).

> The word "revived" could be compared to spring-time. During the winter months, a chill hangs in the air, the grass appears dead, the trees are bare, and no flowers are in sight. Then the weather turns warm, and the rains begin. Everything becomes green again, with splashes of color from flowers blooming here and there. The earth and trees retain life through the winter, but they need the sun and rain to be revived in the spring. Even so, the Philippians' concern for Paul had never died, but it needed the right conditions to blossom again. (28)

You were indeed concerned for me, but you had no opportunity indicates that they were legitimately hindered, and were not being derelict. We are not told in what way they were hindered. Perhaps they did not have funds, had no messenger to bring the funds, or had lost touch with Paul.

> He had not been out of their thoughts, but he had been beyond their reach! When, however, opportunity arose, their thoughts blossomed into action! (29)

11) Not that I am speaking of being in need, for I have learned in whatever situation I am to be content.

Paul issued a disclaimer of sorts. His rejoicing was not dependent on having his needs relieved. **I have learned** indicates that Paul's attitude of contentment was acquired, not inherited. He had to work on it! Through past experiences, he learned how to be content. **Content** or satisfied (see NCV).

12) I know how to be brought low, and I know how to abound. In any and every circumstance, I have learned the secret of facing plenty and hunger, abundance and need.

I know parallels "I have learned" in verse 11, and indicates something known by past experiences. **Brought low** refers to humble circumstances in life (poverty, persecution, imprisonment, isolation, etc). **Abound** refers to prosperous circumstances in life (Roman citizen, student of Gamaliel, etc). **I have learned the secret** comes from a single Greek word *(memyemai)* and was used of pagan initiations. The NEB says "I have been very thoroughly initiated." **Hunger** denotes prolonged, intense hunger. This Greek word was used of Jesus after He had fasted for forty days (Matthew 4:2). Paul often included hunger as one of the things he suffered for the gospel (1 Corinthians 4:11; 2 Corinthians 11:27).

13) I can do all things through him who strengthens me.

Paul now identified the source of his strength--Jesus Christ. **All things** refers to the various circumstances that one might face in life. **Him** is Christ. **Strengthens** means empowers.

95

14) Yet it was kind of you to share my trouble.

Paul was grateful that they sent to his needs. **Trouble** refers to the hardship Paul was facing as a prisoner at Rome.

15) And you Philippians yourselves know that in the beginning of the gospel, when I left Macedonia, no church entered into partnership with me in giving and receiving, except you only.

As he did in 1:5, Paul acknowledged the Philippians financial partnership in the gospel. **You Philippians yourselves know** indicates common knowledge. Paul was reminding them of something they already knew. **Philippians** refers to them by their location. They lived in Philippi. Similarly, Paul referred to the saints at Corinth as "Corinthians" (2 Corinthians 6:11) and the saints in the province of Galatia as "Galatians" (Galatians 3:1). **The beginning of the gospel** refers to their beginning in the gospel. The NIV says "in the early days of your acquaintance with the gospel." Paul was a seasoned soldier in the gospel by the time he reached Philippi.

> Paul certainly did not view his work in Philippi as the beginning point of his ministry as an apostle. He already had about fifteen years of experience before coming to Philippi, having proclaimed Christ in Arabia, Syria, Judea, Cilicia, Cyprus, and Galatia (Acts 9:19-20, 28-30; 11:25-26; 13:4-6, 13-14; 14:1, 8, 20-21; Gal. 1:15-24). However, after he left Philippi, the gospel was new to the Philippian believers. (30)

Macedonia was the Roman province where Philippi was located. It was situated north of Achaia. **Church** is from the Greek word *ekklesia*, and is used here in its local sense (see 3:6). No other congregation sent financial support to Paul when he first left the province. In the next verse Paul said that they even sent to his needs while still in the province. **Partnership** refers to their financial support.

It is important to note that the Philippian church sent their financial support directly to Paul. They did not use a human institution to distribute the funds nor were there any other churches involved. This is the consistent pattern in the New Testament.

16) Even in Thessalonica you sent me help for my needs once and again.

Thessalonica was the capital of the province of Macedonia, and was located about 90 miles from Philippi along the Egnatian Way. After being persecuted in Philippi, Paul traveled to Thessalonica. He did not take money from the Thessalonians while he labored among them, choosing rather to work to support himself (1 Thessalonians 2:9; 2 Thessalonians 3:8). He did, however, receive contributions from the Philippians. **Once and again** means more than once. The phrase is not necessarily limited to twice.

17) Not that I seek the gift, but I seek the fruit that increases to your credit.

Paul was not angling for more support. He was not motivated by greed. **The gift** is financial support. **The fruit that increases to your credit** refers to the spiritual benefits they will reap. The CEB says "a profit that accumulates in your account."

18) I have received full payment, and more. I am well supplied, having received from Epaphroditus the gifts you sent, a fragrant offering, a sacrifice acceptable and pleasing to God.

This verse served as Paul's receipt of payment. **I have received full payment, and more** means that he had received all that they had sent, and it supplied his needs and more. **A fragrant offering** described their gift as a sacrifice which ascends up to heaven as a sweet-smelling aroma (see Hebrews 13:15-16). **A sacrifice acceptable and pleasing to God** means that it was welcomed by God.

19) And my God will supply every need of yours according to his riches in glory in Christ Jesus.

Rather than mentioning his own benefit of their gift, he mentioned their benefit. By giving they would receive. Paul assured them that God would supply the supplier (Galatians 6:7). **My God** emphasizes the close relationship that Paul had with the Father (see 1:3). **Supply** or satisfy. **Every need** refers to physical necessities. **In glory**, that is, in keeping with His glory. **In Christ Jesus** is the sphere.

20) To our God and Father be glory forever and ever. Amen.

Paul now included the Philippians in the close relationship with God. "My" becomes "our." **To our God and Father be glory** is reminiscent of 1:11, where Paul spoke of "the glory and praise of God." **Forever and ever** means for all eternity. **Amen** means so be it.

21) Greet every saint in Christ Jesus. The brothers who are with me greet you.

Every saint refers to all the Philippian brethren; none were excluded. This greeting often included the customary kiss (Romans 16:16; 1 Corinthians 16:20; 2 Corinthians 13:12; 1 Thessalonians 5:26; 1 Peter 5:14). **The brothers who are with me** refers to Timothy and other Christians assisting the apostle in Rome.

22) All the saints greet you, especially those of Caesar's household.

Caesar's household refers to those who served in Caesar's household, including imperial guardsmen, hired servants, and slaves. It may even refer to members of Nero's own family. This shows the effectiveness of Paul's ministry while in chains.

23) The grace of the Lord Jesus Christ be with your spirit.

Paul ended the letter the way it began, with a "grace" blessing (1:2). Paul often concluded his letters by wishing grace upon the readers (Romans 16:20; 1 Corinthians 16:23; Galatians 6:18; Colossians 4:18; 1 Thessalonians 5:28; 2 Thessalonians 3:18; 2

Timothy 4:22; Titus 3:15; Philemon 25). Some manuscripts add the word "Amen" at this point.

FOOTNOTES

(1) Findlay, p. 116

(2) Lipscomb, p. 155

(3) Robertson, Vol. IV, p. 436

(4) Earle, p. 330

(5) Roper, p. 396

(6) Hendriksen, p. 69

(7) Roper, p. 403

(8) Stewart, p. 189

(9) Jackson, p. 52

(10) Wiersbe, p. 69

(11) Kent Jr., p. 115

(12) Vincent, p. 426

(13) Stewart, p. 266

(14) ISBE, Vol. 2, p. 761

(15) The Works of Josephus, Antiquities, Book 18, ch. 3, p. 480

(16) Stewart, p. 293

(17) Vincent, Vol. 3, p. 437

(18) Earle, p. 339

(19) Stewart, p. 314

(20) Foxe's Book of Martyrs, p. 14

(21) Wiersbe, p. 81

(22) Jackson, p. 98

(23) Robertson, IV, p. 451

(24) Stewart, p. 373

(25) Robertson, Vol. 4, pp. 454-455

(26) Stewart, p. 420

(27) Stewart, p. 478

(28) Roper, pp. 560-561

(29) Jackson, pp. 150-151

(30) Stewart, p. 518

Made in the USA
Columbia, SC
05 June 2021